ISBN 0-8373-6729-8
CS-29   GENERAL APTITUDE AND ABILITY SERIES

This is your
PASSBOOK® *for...*

General Aptitude Test (Battery)

Test Preparation Study Guide

Questions & Answers

NATIONAL LEARNING CORPORATION

PLASTIC BOUND—
LIES FLAT FOR
STUDY EASE!

• Easy To Use
• All Tests
• No Fillers

ISBN 0-8373-6729-8

CS-29   GENERAL APTITUDE AND ABILITIES SERIES

This is your
PASSBOOK® for...

General Aptitude Test (Battery)

Test Preparation Study Guide

Questions & Answers

NLC JUN DUMO.

NATIONAL LEARNING CORPORATION

Copyright © 2003 by

National Learning Corporation

212 Michael Drive, Syosset, New York 11791

(516) 921-8888
Outside N.Y.: 1(800) 645-6337
ORDER FAX: 1(516) 921-8743
www.passbooks.com
email: passbooks @ aol.com

PRINTED IN THE UNITED STATES OF AMERICA

PASSBOOK®

NOTICE

PASSBOOK SERIES®

THE *PASSBOOK SERIES*® has been created to prepare applicants and candidates for the ultimate academic battlefield—the examination room.

At some time in our lives, each and every one of us may be required to take an examination—for validation, matriculation, admission, qualification, registration, certification, or licensure.

Based on the assumption that every applicant or candidate has met the basic formal educational standards, has taken the required number of courses, and read the necessary texts, the *PASSBOOK SERIES*® furnishes the one special preparation which may assure passing with confidence, instead of failing with insecurity. Examination questions— together with answers—are furnished as the basic vehicle for study so that the mysteries of the examination and its compounding difficulties may be eliminated or diminished by a sure method.

This book is meant to help you pass your examination provided that you qualify and are serious in your objective.

The entire field is reviewed through the huge store of content information which is succinctly presented through a provocative and challenging approach—the question-and-answer method.

A climate of success is established by furnishing the correct answers at the end of each test.

You soon learn to recognize types of questions, forms of questions, and patterns of questioning. You may even begin to anticipate expected outcomes.

You perceive that many questions are repeated or adapted so that you gain acute insights, which may enable you to score many sure points.

You learn how to confront new questions, or types of questions, and to attack them confidently and work out the correct answers.

You note objectives and emphases, and recognize pitfalls and dangers, so that you may make positive educational adjustments.

Moreover, you are kept fully informed in relation to new concepts, methods, practices, and directions in the field.

You discover that you are actually taking the examination all the time: you are preparing for the examination by "taking" an examination, not by reading extraneous and/or supererogatory textbooks.

In short, this PASSBOOK®, used directedly, should be an important factor in helping you to pass your test.

SAMPLE QUESTIONS

It is important that all candidates study the instructions and questions on this form before the day of the examination.   No samples will be provided in the examination room except for the abstract reasoning questions.

Each question has five suggested answers lettered A, B, C, D, and E.   Decide which one is the best answer to the question.   On the Sample Answer Sheet, find the answer space numbered the same as the question and darken completely the box lettered the same as the best suggested answer.   Then compare your answers with the answers given in the Correct Answers to Sample Questions.   Use the blank spaces on this sheet as scratch paper.   During the examination, use the blank spaces in the test booklet as scratch paper.

Sample Questions 1 through 4—*Verbal Abilities*

1. MANDATORY means most nearly
   A) basic
   B) obligatory
   C) discretionary
   D) discriminatory
   E) advisory

2. SURVEILLANCE means most nearly
   A) continued confinement
   B) indefinite parole
   C) constant protection
   D) unwarranted suspicion
   E) close supervision

3. (*Reading*) "Whenever two groups of people whose interests at the moment conflict meet to discuss a solution of that conflict, there is laid the basis for an interchange of facts and ideas which increases the total range of knowledge of both parties and tends to break down the barrier which their restricted field of information has helped to create."

   Select the alternative that is best supported by the quotation.   Conflicts between two parties may be brought closer to a settlement through
   A) frank acknowledgment of error
   B) the exchange of accusations
   C) gaining a wider knowledge of facts
   D) submitting the dispute to an impartial judge
   E) limiting discussion to plans acceptable to both groups

4. (*Reading*) "One of the primary steps in the development of management in any enterprise is proper organization.   After the business has been conceived and the broad policies that are to be pursued have been established, before any operating methods may be devised, at least a skeleton organization must be developed."

   Select the alternative that is best supported by the quotation.   In industry, some kind of organization is necessary in order that
   A) the type of enterprise may be decided upon
   B) policies may be established
   C) routine work may be planned
   D) capital may be invested
   E) a manager may be selected

SAMPLE ANSWER SHEET

CORRECT ANSWERS TO SAMPLE QUESTIONS

Sample Questions 5 through 9—*Abstract Reasoning*

In each of these questions, look at the symbols in the first two boxes. Something about the three symbols in the first box makes them alike; something about the two symbols in the other box with the question mark makes them alike. Look for some characteristic that is common to all symbols in the same box, yet makes them different from the symbols in the other box. Among the five answer choices, find the symbol that can best be substituted for the question mark, because it is *like* the symbols in the second box, and, *for the same reason*, different from those in the first box.

In question 5, all the symbols in the first box are curved lines. The second box has two lines, one dotted and one solid. Their *likeness* to each other consists in their straightness; and this straightness makes them *different* from the curves in the other box. The answer must be the *only* one of the five lettered choices that is a straight line, either dotted or solid. Now do questions 6 through 9.

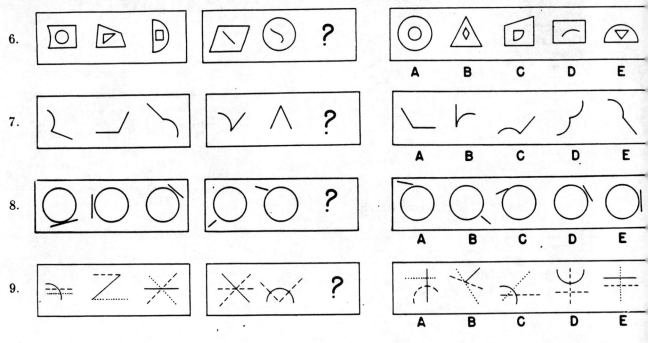

NOTE.—There is not supposed to be a *series* or progression in these symbol questions. If you look for a progression in the first box and try to find the missing figure to fill out a similar progression in the second box, you will be wasting time. For example, look at question 5. A competitor who saw that both boxes had a horizontal figure followed by an oblique one might try to find a vertical figure to match the last one in the first box. If he chose D he would be missing the real point of the question. Remember, look for a *likeness* within each box and a *difference* between the two boxes.

SAMPLE ANSWER SHEET						CORRECT ANSWERS TO SAMPLE QUESTIONS				
A	B	C	D	E		A	B	C	D	E
5						5	■			
A	B	C	D	E		A	B	C	D	E
6						6				■
A	B	C	D	E		A	B	C	D	E
7						7	■			
A	B	C	D	E		A	B	C	D	E
8						8	■			
A	B	C	D	E		A	B	C	D	E
9						9			■	

2

POPULATION MOVEMENT TO AND FROM COUNTY X
1943 TO 1964

MOVING TO COUNTY ----------
MOVING FROM COUNTY ————

SAMPLE ANSWER SHEET

CORRECT ANSWERS TO SAMPLE QUESTIONS

10. The graph above indicates that, with respect to County X, migratory activities during the period from 1943 to 1964 tended mostly to result in
A) population gains
B) population losses
C) gradual stabilization of population
D) irregular fluctuations in population without consistent direction
E) cycles of alternating losses and gains in population which tended to balance each other

11. According to the table below, which industry division showed the greatest percentage increase from 1945 to 1960?
A) Contract Construction
B) Manufacturing
C) Trade
D) Service
E) Government

EMPLOYEES IN NONAGRICULTURAL ESTABLISHMENTS BY INDUSTRY, 1940–1960

(In thousands)

Industry Division	1940	1945	1950	1955	1960
Mining	916	826	901	792	712
Contract Construction	1,294	1,132	2,333	2,802	2,885
Manufacturing	10,870	15,302	15,241	16,882	16,796
Transportation and Public Utilities	3,013	3,872	4,034	4,141	4,004
Trade	6,940	7,522	9,386	10,535	11,391
Finance	1,419	1,394	1,919	2,335	2,669
Service	3,477	4,055	5,382	6,274	7,392
Government	4,192	5,967	6,026	6,914	8,520

HOW TO TAKE A TEST

You have studied hard, long, and conscientiously.

With your official admission card in hand, and your heart pounding, you have been admitted to the examination room.

You note that there are several hundred other applicants in the examination room waiting to take the same test.

They all appear to be equally well prepared.

You know that nothing but your best effort will suffice. The "moment of truth" is at hand: you now have to demonstrate objectively, in writing, your knowledge of content and your understanding of subject matter.

You are fighting the most important battle of your life — to pass and/or score high on an examination which will determine your career and provide the economic basis for your livelihood.

What extra, special things should you know and should you do in taking the examination?

BEFORE THE TEST

YOUR PHYSICAL CONDITION IS IMPORTANT

If you are not well, you can't do your best work on tests. If you are half asleep, you can't do your best either. Here are some tips:

1. Get about the same amount of sleep you usually get. Don't stay up all night before the test, either partying or worrying — DON'T DO IT.

2. If you wear glasses, be sure to wear them when you go to take the test. This goes for hearing aids, too.

3. If you have any physical problems that may keep you from doing your best, be sure to tell the person giving the test. If you are sick or in poor health, you really cannot do your best on any test. You can always come back and take the test some other time.

AT THE TEST

EXAMINATION TECHNIQUES

1. Read the *general* instructions carefully. These are usually printed on the first page of the examination booklet. As a rule, these instructions refer to the timing of the examination; the fact that you should not start work until the signal and must stop work at a signal, etc. If there are any *special* instructions, such as a choice of questions to be answered, make sure that you note this instruction carefully.

2. **When you are ready to start work on the examination,** that is as soon as the signal has been given, read the instructions to each question booklet, underline any key words or phrases, such as *least, best, outline, describe,* and the like. In this way you will tend to answer as requested rather than discover on reviewing your paper that you *listed without describing,* that you selected the *worst* choice rather than the *best* choice, etc.

3. If the examination is of the objective or so-called multiple-choice type, that is, each question will also give a series of possible answers: A, B, C, or D, and you are called upon to select the best answer and write the letter next to that answer on your answer paper, it is advisable to start answering each question in turn. There may be anywhere from 50 to 100 such questions in the three or four hours allotted and you can see how much time would be taken if you read through all the questions before beginning to answer any. Furthermore, if you come across a question or a group of questions which you know would be difficult to answer, it would undoubtedly affect your handling of all the other questions.

4. If the examination is of the essay-type and contains but a few questions, it is a moot point as to whether you should read all the questions before starting to answer any one. Of course if you are given a choice, say five out of seven and the like, then it is essential to read all the questions so you can eliminate the two which are most difficult. If, however, you are asked to answer all the questions, there may be danger in trying to answer the easiest one first because you may find that you will spend too much time on it. The best technique is to answer the first question, then proceed to the second, etc.

5. Time your answers. Before the examination begins, write down the time it started, then add the time allowed for the examination and write down the time it must be completed, then divide the time available somewhat as follows:

   a. If 3½ hours are allowed, that would be 210 minutes. If you have 80 objective-type questions, that would be an average of about 2½ minutes per question. Allow yourself no more than 2 minutes per question, or a total of 160 minutes, which will permit about 50 minutes to review.

   b. If for the time allotment of 210 minutes, there are 7 essay questions to answer, that would average about 30 minutes a question. Give yourself only 25 minutes per question so that you have about 35 minutes to review.

6. **The most important instruction is** *to read each question* **and make sure you know what is wanted.** The second most important instruction is to *time yourself properly* so that you answer every question. The third most important instruction is to *answer every question.* Guess if you have to but include something for each question, Remember that you will receive no credit for a blank and will probably receive some credit if you write something in answer to an essay question. If you guess a letter, say "B" for a multiple-choice question, you may have guessed right. If you leave a blank as the answer to a multiple-choice question, the examiners may respect your feelings but it will not add a point to your score. Some exams may penalize you for wrong answers, so in such cases *only*, you may not want to guess unless you have some basis for your answer.

7. Suggestions

   a. Objective-Type Questions

      (1) Examine the question booklet for proper sequence of pages and questions.

      (2) Read all instructions carefully.

      (3) Skip any question which seems too difficult; return to it after all other questions have been answered.

      (4) Apportion your time properly; do not spend too much time on any single question or group of questions.

      (5) Note and underline key words — *all, most, fewest, least, best, worst, same, opposite.*

      (6) Pay particular attention to negatives.

      (7) Note unusual option, e.g., unduly long, short, complex, different or similar in content to the body of the question.

      (8) Observe the use of "hedging" words — *probably, may, most likely, etc.*

      (9) Make sure that your answer is put next to the same number as the question.

      (10) Do not second guess unless you have good reason to believe the second answer is definitely more correct.

      (11) Cross out original answer if you decide another answer is more accurate; do not erase, *until* you are ready to hand your paper in.

      (12) Answer all questions; guess unless instructed otherwise.

      (13) Leave time for review.

b. Essay-Type Questions

   (1) Read each question carefully.

   (2) Determine exactly what is wanted. Underline key words or phrases.

   (3) Decide on outline or paragraph answer.

   (4) Include many different points and elements unless asked to develop any one or two points or elements.

   (5) Show impartiality by giving pros and cons unless directed to select one side only.

   (6) Make and write down any assumptions you find necessary to answer the question.

   (7) Watch your English, grammar, punctuation, choice of words.

   (8) Time your answers; don't crowd material.

8. Answering the Essay Question

   Most essay questions can be answered by framing the specific response around several key words or ideas. Here are a few such key words or ideas:

   M's: manpower, materials, methods, money, management

   P's: purpose, program, policy, plan, procedure, practice, problems, pitfalls, personnel, public relations

   a. Six basic steps in handling problems:

   (1) preliminary plan and background development

   (2) collect information, data and facts

   (3) analyze and interpret information, data and facts

   (4) analyze and develop solutions as well as make recommendations

   (5) prepare report and sell recommendations

   (6) install recommendations and follow up effectiveness

   b. Pitfalls to Avoid

   (1) *Taking Things for Granted*
   A statement of the situation does not necessarily imply that each of the elements is necessarily true; for example, a complaint may be invalid and biased so that all that can be taken for granted is that a complaint has been registered

   (2) *Considering only one side of a situation*
   Wherever possible, indicate several alternatives and then point out the reasons you selected the best one.

   (3) *Failing to indicate follow up*
   Whenever your answer indicates action on your part, make certain that you will take proper follow-up action to see how successful your recommendations, procedures, or actions turn out to be.

   (4) *Taking too long in answering any single question*
   Remember to time your answers properly.

EXAMINATION SECTION

EXAMINATION SECTION
COMMENTARY

This section illustrates the different types of questions in a written test of general aptitude and competency. These questions are similar to actual questions in difficulty, content, and form. Competitors should carefully study every question so that they are prepared for questions of the same type in the examination. Some difficult questions are included in this section and competitors should not be discouraged if they miss some of them. No applicant is expected to answer all questions correctly on the written test.

The written test consists of several sections which measure the abilities that are considered essential in carrying out the duties of the positions filled through this examination.

QUESTIONS AND ANSWERS

EXPLANATION OF ANSWERS

DIRECTIONS: Each question or incorrect answer is followed by several suggested answers or completions. Select the one that BEST answers the question or completes the statement.

Question-type 1
    Many jobs require the ability to analyze, understand, and interpret written material of varying levels of complexity and to retain the content for at least a limited period of time. Question-type 1 is primarily designed to test these comprehension and retention abilities. The following questions, therefore, require competitors to understand a given paragraph and to select an answer based on their comprehension of the conceptual content of the paragraph. The right answer is either
    (1) a repetition, formulated in different terminology, of the main concept or concepts found in the paragraph, or
    (2) a conclusion whose inherence in the content of the paragraph is such that it is equivalent to a restatement.

----

1. Through advertising, manufacturers exercise a high degree of control over consumers' desires. However, the manufacturer assumes enormous risks in attempting to predict what consumers will want and in producing goods in quantity and distributing them in advance of final selection by the consumers.

The paragraph best supports the statement that manufacturers

A) can eliminate the risk of overproduction by advertising
B) completely control buyers' needs and desires
C) must depend upon the final consumers for the success of their undertakings
D) distribute goods directly to the consumers
E) can predict with great accuracy the success of any product they put on the market

The conclusion derived by the correct alternative, C, is inherent in the content of the paragraph; although it acknowledges that advertising plays an important role in determining consumers' desires, it affirms that final selection rests with the consumers and that manufacturers therefore take *enormous* risks in attempting to predict final selection. Alternative B contradicts the opening sentence of the paragraph which refers only to a "high degree of control." Alternatives A and E likewise affirm the opposite of what the paragraph postulates, i.e., that the manufacturer's predictions entail enormous risks. Alternative D is almost irrelevant to the paragraph since distribution techniques have not been considered.

2. The function of business is to increase the wealth of the country and the value and happiness of life. It does this by supplying the material needs of men and women. When the nation's business is successfully carried on, it renders public service of the highest value.

The paragraph best supports the statement that

A) all businesses which render public service are successful
B) human happiness is enhanced only by the increase of material wants
C) the value of life is increased only by the increase of wealth
D) the material needs of men and women are supplied by well-conducted business
E) business is the only field of activity which increases happiness

The correct alternative, D, restates the main idea in the original paragraph that business increases the value and happiness of life by supplying the material needs of men and women. Alternative A derives its conclusion incorrectly, i.e., the proposition that all successful businesses render public service, cannot be logically reversed to "all businesses which render public service are successful." Alternatives B and C assume an equation between happiness and wealth which is not supported by the content of the paragraph. Alternative E likewise equates happiness with business endeavors or their products, which the content of the paragraph does not warrant.

3. Honest people in one nation find it difficult to understand the viewpoints of honest people in another. Foreign ministries and their ministers exist for the purpose of explaining the viewpoints of one nation in terms understood by the ministries of another. Some of their most important work lies in this direction.

The paragraph best supports the statement that

A) people of different nations may not consider matters in the same light
B) it is unusual for many people to share similar ideas
C) suspicion prevents understanding between nations
D) the chief work of foreign ministries is to guide relations between nations united by a common cause
E) the people of one nation must sympathize with the viewpoints of the people of other nations

The conclusion derived by the correct alternative, A, is inherent in the content of the paragraph; if honest people in one nation find it difficult to understand the viewpoints of honest people in another, it is because they often see matters in different lights. Alternatives B, C and D find little or no support in the paragraph: B is concerned with "many people" whereas the paragraph refers to people of different nations; C *assumes* that nations are suspicious of each other and that suspicion prevents understanding; D contradicts the main idea expressed by the paragraph since foreign ministries should work towards mutual understanding between nations having discrepant viewpoints whether or not they have a common cause. Alternative E sets forth an ethical command which to an extent stems from the content of the paragraph but which is not completely warranted by it as is the conclusion of alternative A.

4. Education should not stop when the individual has been prepared to make a livelihood and to live in modern society. Living would be mere existence were there no appreciation and enjoyment of the riches of art, literature and science.

The paragraph best supports the statement that true education
A) is focused on the routine problems of life
B) prepares one for a full enjoyment of life
C) deals chiefly with art, literature and science
D) is not possible for one who does not enjoy scientific literature
E) disregards practical ends

The correct alternative, B, restates the main idea presented in the paragraph that living is mere existence for those individuals who lack the enjoyment of art, literature and science. Alternative A directly contradicts this main idea, and alternatives C and E also contradict the paragraph which acknowledges that education should prepare the individual to make a livelihood although it shouldn't stop there. Alternative D goes beyond the paragraph in that it affirms that each individual *must* enjoy scientific literature whereas the original statement simply suggests that life in general would be limited if the riches of science, art and literature were not available for appreciation and enjoyment.

Question-type II
Many _____ jobs require the use of clear and succinct verbal and written expression. Basic vocabulary limitations impede the precise correspondence of words and concepts and thus hinder effective language communication. Accordingly, the following questions present a key word and five suggested answers. The competitor's task is to find the suggested answer that is closest in meaning to the key word. The wrong alternatives may have a more or less valid connection with the key word. In some cases, therefore, the right choice differs from a wrong choice only in the degree to which its meaning comes close to that of the key word.

1. *Subsume* means most nearly
   A) understate
   B) absorb
   C) include
   D) belong
   E) cover

To *subsume* means to include within a larger class or order (alternative C). Alternative A is unrelated in meaning. Alternatives D and E are somewhat related since an element included in a group or class can be said to belong to it and to be covered by it. To a degree, likewise, it may be said that an element included in a group or class is absorbed (alternative B) by the group or class, although strictly speaking, a subsumed element partially preserves its individual identity whereas an absorbed element does not.

2. *Notorious* means most nearly
   A) condemned
   B) unpleasant
   C) vexatious
   D) pretentious
   E) well-known

Notorious means being or constituting something commonly known. Thus alternative E is almost synonymous in meaning. Alternatives B, C and D are unrelated in meaning, since a notorious individual may or may not be unpleasant, vexatious or pretentious. Alternative A hinges on a secondary nuance of the word notorious: being widely and unfavorably known. However, being unfavorably well-known does not necessarily imply being condemned.

3. *Novices* means most nearly
   A) volunteers
   B) experts
   C) trainers
   D) beginners
   E) amateurs

Novice designates one who has no training or experience in a specific field or activity and is hence a beginner (alternative D). An expert (alternative B) is therefore the exact opposite. A trainer (alternative C) may or may not be an expert but must certainly have a certain amount of knowledge. Volunteers (alternative A) are in most cases not novices since they usually volunteer for something they are knowledgeable in. An amateur (alternative E) is one who engages in a particular pursuit, study or science as a pastime rather than as a profession. Thus an amateur may be a novice in the initial stages of formal training, but more often than not will be an expert who has acquired expertise in a particular field through the consistent pursuit of a pastime or pleasure.

4. To *succumb* means most nearly
   A) to aid
   B) to oppose
   C) to yield
   D) to check
   E) to be discouraged

To *succumb* is to cease to resist or contend before a superior or overpowering force or desire, hence to yield (alternative C). Alternative B expresses the stage prior to succumbing.

Alternative A is not related except perhaps accidentally—an individual who succumbs may involuntarily serve the purpose of the overpowering force. Alternative D is unrelated in meaning, and alternative E is related only vaguely in the sense that the succumbing party may be susceptible to discouragement.

Question-type III
The ability to discover the underlying relations or analogies existing among specific data is important in many   jobs where solving problems involves the formation and testing of hypotheses. The questions in this section test this ability. Each question consists of a series of letters arranged in a definite pattern. The competitor must discover what the pattern is and decide which alternative gives the next letter in the series.

1. b c d b c e b c f b c g

A) b B) c C) h D) i E) e

The answer is A. The sequence maintains two letters (b c) in the same order while the third letter is in consecutive alphabetical order (d e f g). The pattern b c g has been completed and the next letter should begin the pattern b c h.

2. b c c c d e e e f g g g h i i

A) g B) h C) i D) j E) f

The answer is C. The pattern consists of letters written in alphabetical order with every second letter repeated three times. Since the last letter in the sequence, the i, is only repeated twice, it should be repeated a third time.

3. b n c d n e f g n h i j k

A) n B) l C) m D) i E) j

The answer is A. The sequence consists of a fixed letter (n) placed after consecutive letter periods. These periods acquire an additional letter each time and begin with the letter which alphabetically follows the last letter in the preceding period, i.e., *bn cdn efgn hijk*. The letter n must therefore be placed after the last period.

4. b c d b e f g e h i j h k l m

A) k B) h C) l D) n E) o

The answer is A. The series is an alphabetical progression of four-letter sequences where each fourth letter repeats the first letter of each sequence: *bcdb efge hijh klmk*.

Question-type IV
As in the previous section the questions in this section measure the ability to discover the underlying relations or analogies existing among specific data. Each question consists of two sets of symbols where a common characteristic exists among the symbols in each set and where an analogy is maintained between the two sets of symbols. The competitor must discover which alternative gives the symbol that simultaneously preserves the characteristic common to the symbols in the second set and the analogy with the symbols in the first set.

1.

The answer is C. An analogy is established here between a circle and a square. Therefore a circle split into two halves is the same as a square split into two halves.

2.

The answer is B. In this case the form of the symbols is irrelevant. The critical feature is found in the lines included within the symbols. The lines in the first three symbols are all slanted lines. The lines in the second two symbols are all vertical lines. Of the five alternatives, symbol B is the only one with vertical lines.

4

3.

The answer is E. The symbols in the first box are made up of straight lines. The symbols in the second box are made up of curved lines.

The symbol in alternative E is the only one that preserves the pattern.

4.

The answer is C. The first three symbols are identical except for their orientation—the orientation of the second symbol is a 90° rotation of the first symbol. Likewise the third symbol is a

90° rotation of the second symbol. The symbols in the second box follow the same 90° rotation pattern. Alternative C is the only one that preserves the pattern.

Question-type V
The development of plans, systems and procedures is an essential function of many jobs. This function entails the ability to analyze given facts and discover their implications, as well as the ability to reason from general principles to the implications of these principles in specific situations. Question-type V tests these analytical abilities. Accordingly, each of the following questions consists of a statement which is to be accepted as true and should not be questioned for the purpose of this test. Following the statement are five alternatives. The correct alternative MUST derive from the information given in the original statement without drawing on additional information. By contrast, the four incorrect alternatives rest, to varying degrees, on the admission of new information.

1. No substantial alterations in the age structure took place between 1960-70 and life expectancy remained the same. A slight drop, nonetheless (from 38 to 37 per cent), is noted in the proportion of the population 20 years of age and younger.
   Therefore, between 1960-70
   A) the proportion of the productive-age population increased
   B) there was a slight decrease in fertility rates
   C) there was a decrease in emigration
   D) there was a slight increase in infant mortality
   E) production remained substantially the same

The correct alternative, A, follows from the data that there was a slight drop in the proportion of the population under 20 years of age and that life expectancy remained the same. Alternatives B and D are possible explanations of the slight decrease in the proportion of the younger population but do not derive from the original statement and would require additional evidence. Alternative C would likewise require additional information and would seem to apply more as a partial and possible explanation of a decrease in the productive-age population. Alternative E in no way derives from the given data since many factors affect production besides the age structure of the population.

2. A robot can take a walk in order to mail a letter; it can play chess, build other machines and generally exhibit rule-governed behavior. A robot can kill a person but, unlike a person, it cannot be ashamed. It can be annoying but not annoyed. It can *perhaps* exhibit behavior *as if* it were ashamed or annoyed.
   A) Robots are capable of thought.
   B) Robots can do things that people do but cannot be what people are.
   C) Robots and people are outwardly the same.
   D) Robots can make conscious decisions but have no moral consciousness.
   E) Robots never exhibit their inner thoughts and realities.

The correct alternative, B, derives its conclusion from the joint consideration of the actions enumerated in the original statement as actions that a robot can perform—mailing a letter, playing chess, killing a person—and the conscious states that are enumerated as impossible in a robot, i.e., being ashamed or annoyed. Furthermore, the last sentence in the original statement contrasts outward behaviors with the actual conscious states they represent. Alternative A rests on the assumption that thought can be equated with exhibited behavior and not with inner consciousness. Alternative C assumes not only that all exhibited behavior is the same but that the outward *appearance* of a robot and a person is the same. Alternative D correctly derives a section of its conclusion—the lack of moral consciousness—from the stated fact that a robot cannot be ashamed, but assumes that a robot can kill a person after making a *conscious* decision, which contradicts the original statement. Alternative E likewise affirms, in contradiction of the original statement, that robots have inner consciousness.

3. The Thirty Years' War, 1618 to 1648, established the principle of religious toleration among the German states, but it also reduced the German population by at least one-third, and much of the cultivated land became wilderness.
   Therefore, the Thirty Years' War
   A) altered the geographical boundaries of the German states
   B) was generally beneficial to the German states
   C) was fought on German soil
   D) established a large number of religions within the German states
   E) caused the German population to become widely scattered

The correct alternative, C, derives its conclusion from the given facts that the German population was reduced by one-third and much of the cultivated land became wilderness. Alternative A, on the other hand, assumes the establishment of new borders from the extraneous information that borders are usually changed by wars. Alternative B derives its conclusion from the assumption that religious tolerance creates a surrounding influence beneficial to all aspects of national life. Alternative D assumes an equation between religious tolerance and religious pluralism, and alternative E likewise assumes an equation between the reduction of the population and the scattering of the population.

4. Though easy to learn, backgammon is a surprisingly subtle and complex game to play very well. It is a game that calls for mastery of the laws of probability and the ability to weigh and undertake frequent shifts in strategy.
   Therefore, a necessary quality for playing backgammon very well is
   A) the ability to deceive the opponent
   B) a willingness to take calculated risks
   C) a high degree of manual dexterity
   D) the ability to make quick decisions
   E) a mastery of advanced mathematics

The correct alternative, B, derives its conclusion from the given fact that the game is based on decisions of probability. Thus the player must take calculated risks. The four incorrect alternatives, on the other hand, rest on assumptions that, to varying degrees, go beyond the original statement. Alternative E, for example, assumes that a mastery of the laws of probability entails a more generic mastery of advanced mathematics. Alternative D assumes that frequent shifts in strategy cannot be carried out slowly.

Question-type VI

Many _____ jobs require the ability to understand and utilize information presented in chart or table form. The following questions require competitors to deduce the missing values in a table of figures from the information in the rest of the table.

TABLE I: GENERAL REVENUE OF STATE AND LOCAL GOVERNMENTS—STATES: 1970
Hypothetical data

STATE	Total amount (mil. dol.)	REVENUE PER CAPITA [1] (dollars)							REVENUE (dollars) PER $1,000 OF PERSONAL INCOME IN CALENDAR YEAR, 1969:				
		Total	From Federal Government	From own sources					Total	From Federal Government	From own sources		
				Taxes			Charges and miscellaneous						
				All taxes	Property tax	Other					Total	Taxes	Charges and miscellaneous
Ala.	1,722	I	131	258	39	219	110		190	50	140	98	42
Alaska	1,259	4,168	358	417	102	315	3,393		1,001	86	915	II	815
Ariz.	1,172	662	121	426	166	260	115		206	38	168	132	36
Ark.	871	453	115	252	65	187	86		176	45	131	98	33
Calif.	17,028	853	164	559	262	297	130		204	39	165	134	31
Colo.	1,474	666	III	419	179	240	123		194	36	158	122	36
Conn.	1,970	649	85	484	238	246	80		144	19	125	107	18
Del.	379	692	88	450	84	366	154		172	22	150	112	38
D.C.	IV	953	359	517	169	348	77		192	72	120	104	16
Fla.	3,576	528	69	347	118	229	112		160	21	139	105	34

[1] Based on resident population

1. **What is the value of I?**
   A) 800
   B) 600
   C) 499
   D) 757
   E) None of these, or cannot be calculated from data provided

The answer is C. The figure represents the total Revenue per Capita which is obtained by adding the three major columns therein: Charges and miscellaneous, All taxes and Federal Government: 110 + 258 + 131 = 499. Alternative D represents an erroneous double addition of the Property tax and Other subcolumns, the amounts corresponding to which were already included in the All taxes column. Alternatives A and B are irrelevant values.

2. **What is the value of II?**
   A) 392
   B) 828
   C) 100
   D) 1814
   E) None of these, or cannot be calculated from data provided

The answer is C. It is obtained by subtracting Charges and miscellaneous from the Total Revenue from own sources: 915 − 815 = 100. Alternatives A, B and D are irrelevant values.

3. **What is the value of III?**
   A) 124
   B) 141
   C) 176
   D) 203
   E) None of these, or cannot be calculated from data provided

The answer is A. It is obtained by adding the two major columns for which values are given in the Revenue per Capita subdivision, All taxes and Charges and miscellaneous, and subtracting the result from the total Revenue per Capita: 419 + 123 = 542; 666 − 542 = 124. Alternatives B, C and D are irrelevant values.

4. **What is the value of IV?**
   A) 725
   B) 687
   C) 710
   D) 1144
   E) None of these, or cannot be calculated from data provided

The answer is E. The Total General Revenue cannot be calculated, since the total population figure is missing. This figure should be multiplied by the Per Capita Income to obtain the Total Revenue. Alternative D erroneously adds the totals for Revenue per Capita and Revenue per $1,000 of Personal Income: 192 + 953 = 1145. Alternatives A, B and C are irrelevant values.

Many _____ jobs require employees to perform or check arithmetic operations involving fractions, percentages, etc. and to solve quantitative problems of varying complexity, where the approach to be utilized is not specified. The questions in this section test these abilities. Although the arithmetical processes involved are simple, the figuring should of course be done with care.

1. $113^{17}/_{52} - 33^{5}/_{13} =$
   A) $79^{49}/_{52}$
   B) $80^{3}/_{52}$
   C) $80^{12}/_{52}$
   D) $80^{49}/_{52}$
   E) None of these

The answer is A. First of all fractions are reduced to a common denominator. Additionally, since the fraction being subtracted is larger than the one it is to be subtracted from, a unit must be taken from the whole number, 113, reducing it ito 112. The borrowed unit is converted into fraction form and added to 17/52, i.e., $^{52}/_{52} + {^{17}/_{52}} = {^{69}/_{52}}$. The subtraction is then carried out: $112^{69}/_{52} - 33^{20}/_{52} = 79^{49}/_{52}$.

2. $\dfrac{16 \times 17}{(57 + 79)\,4} =$

   A) .50
   B) .72
   C) 1.9
   D) 8.0
   E) None of these

The answer is A. The numbers in parentheses are added, $57 + 79 = 136$ and 136 is then broken into $17 \times 2 \times 4$. Common factors are eliminated:

$$\frac{16 \times 17}{(57 + 79)4} = \frac{16 \times 17}{(136)4} = \frac{16 \times 17}{(17 \times 2 \times 4)4} =$$
$$\frac{16 \times 17}{17 \times 2 \times 4 \times 4} = \frac{1}{2} = .50$$

3. $221^{1}/_{19} \times 10^{11}/_{35} =$

   A) 80.3
   B) 2510.0
   C) 2510.1
   D) 2280
   E) None of these

The answer is D. Whole numbers are reduced to fractions: $\dfrac{4200}{19} \times \dfrac{361}{35}$. Fractions are broken into their component factors and common factors are eliminated: $\dfrac{7 \times 6 \times 100}{19} \times \dfrac{19 \times 19}{7 \times 5} =$

$$\frac{7 \times 6 \times 5 \times 20 \times 19 \times 19}{19 \times 7 \times 5} =$$
$6 \times 20 \times 19 = 2280$.

4. $\dfrac{(418 + 56 - 8)313}{77 + (50 + 9)7 - 24} =$

   A) $-$ 12378
   B) 310
   C) 313
   D) 1246.649
   E) None of these

The answer is C.
$$\frac{(466)(313)}{77 + (59)7 - 24} = \frac{(466)(313)}{77 + 413 - 24} =$$
$$\frac{(466)(313)}{490 - 24} = \frac{(466)(313)}{466}.$$
Common factors are eliminated and the result is 313.

5. An office supply store buys 100 reams of special quality paper for $400. If 1 ream = 500 sheets of paper, how much must the store receive per 100 sheets to obtain a 20% gain on its cost?
   A) 83¢
   B) 85¢
   C) 96¢
   D) 98¢
   E) None of these

The answer is C. Since 1 ream = 500 sheets, 100 reams = 50000 sheets. To discover the cost of 100 sheets we set up a proportion:
$$\frac{50000}{100} = \frac{400}{x}; \ 50000\, x = 40000; \ x = \frac{40000}{50000} =$$
0.80. The cost of 100 sheets is 80¢. To discover the amount that the store must receive per 100 sheets to obtain a 20% gain on the 80¢ cost, we find what 20% of 80¢ is and add the result: $80 + (0.20)(80) = 80 + 16 = 96$¢.

6. A vase is packed in a carton with a 10″ diameter and is surrounded by packing 2″ thick at the mouth. If the diameter of the base is ½ the diameter of the mouth, what is the diameter of the base?
   A) 3″
   B) 4″
   C) 6″
   D) 8″
   E) None of these

The answer is A. Since the vase is surrounded by packing 2″ thick at the mouth and the diameter of the carton is 10″, we subtract: $10 - (2 + 2) = 10 - 4 = 6$″ which is the diameter of the mouth. Since the diameter of the base is ½ the diameter of the mouth: $½(6) = 3$″.

7. Seventy 58″ × 34″ desks must be stored in a warehouse. If as many desks as possible are stored on the floor of a 15′ × 25′ room, how many desks will still require storage?

   A) 46
   B) 25
   C) 45
   D) 43
   E) None of these

The answer is C. First of all, the feet are reduced to inches: 15 × 12 = 180 and 25 × 12 = 300. Next we determine how many times the length of a desk fits into the length of the room and how many times the width of a desk fits into the width of the room: $\frac{180}{34}=5\frac{10}{34}$ and $\frac{300}{58}=5\frac{10}{58}$. We then multiply the whole numbers, which means multiplying the number of desks per row by the number of rows: 5 × 5 = 25. Since 25 desks fit in the room, 45 desks will still require storage (70 − 25 = 45).

Alternative D is obtained by multiplying the width and length of the room and the width and length of a desk and dividing the total storage area by the total area of a desk: 180 × 300 = 54000 and 58 × 34 = 1972; 54000 ÷ 1972 = $27\frac{189}{493}$. Since 70 − 27 = 43, more desks would fit in the same area. However, this solution is incorrect because it does not take into account that the storage space cannot be filled *completely* with desks. The shape of the desks is not adjustable to the shape of the room and there would always be unfilled spaces. Alternative A is obtained by determining how many times the width of a desk fits into the length of the room and the length of a desk fits into the width of the room: $\frac{300}{34} = 8\frac{14}{17}$ and $\frac{180}{58} = 3\frac{3}{29}$. The multiplication of the whole numbers yields 24, and 70 − 24 = 46. One more desk actually fits into the storage area if we follow the process used to obtain the correct answer, alternative C.

8. A mechanic repairs 16 cars per 8-hour day. Another mechanic in the same shop repairs 1½ times this number in ¾ the time. Theoretically, how long will it take to repair 16 cars in the shop?

   A) 2⅔ hours
   B) 2⁹⁄₁₀ hours
   C) 3 hours
   D) 2½ hours
   E) None of these

The answer is A. For the second mechanic we obtain 1½ of 16 cars: ³⁄₂ × 16 = 24 and ¾ of 8 hours: ¾ × 8 = 6 hours. The second mechanic therefore repairs 24 cars per 6-hour day. Secondly we determine how many cars each mechanic repairs per hour—the first mechanic: 2 cars/hr. and the second mechanic 4 cars/hr. Therefore 6 cars are repaired every hour if both outputs are added. Lastly we determine how many hours are required to repair 16 cars: we divide the 16 cars by the 6 cars/hr. which yields 2⅔ hrs.

Question-type VIII
Many . .   jobs require the ability to solve a presented problem when all the necessary facts to solve the problem are not given. Solution to the problem involves making some reasonable assumptions or anticipating what the most likely of several possible occurrences might be. This ability becomes especially important when decisions must be reached based on incomplete evidence. Accordingly, the questions in this section require competitors to select the best or most reasonable answer from five alternatives. In order to do so, competitors are required to use general knowledge not included in the original statement. Since the correct alternative consists of the best or most reasonable answer, it is essential to keep in mind that some alternatives may be plausible, although not as plausible as the correct alternative.

1. The development of a country's water power is advocated as a means of conserving natural resources CHIEFLY because such a hydroelectric policy would tend to

   A) stimulate the growth of industries in hitherto isolated regions
   B) encourage the substitution of machinery for hand labor
   C) provide a larger market for coal
   D) make cheap electricity available in rural areas
   E) lessen the use of irreplaceable fuel materials

Of the five alternatives, the correct alternative, E, derives from the fundamental or most essential reason for the endorsement of a hydroelectric policy, i.e., water is not a depletable energy resource. Alternatives A and D are plausible but are not as determinative as E. Alternative C is easily discarded since coal would have a larger market in the absence of hydroelectric power. Alternative B is also easily discarded since hydroelectric energy would increase the availability of both the fuel and/or electricity needed to run machinery.

2. Complaints by the owners of large cars that they cannot see an already-parked small car in a parking lot until they have begun to pull into a space, are BEST justified if
   A) there are few empty parking spaces in the lot
   B) the small car has been parked for a long time
   C) the owners of large cars have poor vision
   D) there is a designated parking area for small cars
   E) there are few other small cars in the lot

The correct alternative, D, hinges on the fact that strict *justification* for a complaint is more firmly rooted in legality than in individual situations or attitudes. Thus, for example, the owner of a large car who happens to find few empty parking spaces in a lot (alternative A), or who knows or assumes that a small car has been parked in a certain space for a long time (alternative B), can justify his or her annoyance only on the subjective level. On the other hand if a small car is parked in a space designated for large cars, the individual's annoyance and complaint acquire objective and formal justification.

3. A country that is newly settled usually produces very little art, music or literature. The MOST REASONABLE explanation of this fact is that
   A) its people have had few experiences to draw on
   B) there is little use for such work
   C) suitable materials for such work must be imported
   D) the physical development of the country absorbs most of the interest and energy of the people
   E) there is as yet no governmental encouragement of the arts

The correct alternative, D, presents the most basic explanation for the lack of artistic production in a newly-settled country. The development of a newly-settled country necessitates the undivided attention of its people, and manpower is thus basically unavailable for the production of art, music or literature. Alternative A is implausible since newly-settled people have many experiences which are eventually represented in the art, music and literature of later generations. Alternatives B, C and E make assumptions about conditions necessary for the production of art, music and literature which are only partially valid. Alternative B incorrectly assumes that art is always produced for utilitarian purposes. Alternative C partially applies to art and music but not at all to literature. Alternative E is only partially plausible. The government of a newly-settled country is likely to encourage the production of goods rather than the production of art, music or literature.

However, artistic production can occur without governmental encouragement.

4. The CHIEF reason why every society has certain words and concepts that are never precisely translated into the language of another society is that
   A) the art of good translation is as yet not sufficiently developed
   B) there is too great a disparity between the intellectual levels attained by different societies
   C) every society possesses cultural elements which are unique to itself
   D) words and concepts never express the true nature of a society
   E) every society has some ideas which it does not wish to share with other societies

The correct alternative, C, is the most basic reason why certain concepts are never precisely translated. Languages express the sociopolitical contexts in which they are spoken and are bound to have expressions that are unique to these contexts. Alternative A fails to distinguish between the qualitative and the quantitative. Whereas the art of good translation appears to be as yet not sufficiently widespread, it is indeed available. Furthermore its total unavailability would still constitute a secondary explanation, over and against alternative C, for the impossibility of the precise translation of certain words. Alternative B rests on the assumption that *all* existing societies are substantially disparate in their level of development, which is known not to be the case. Alternative D assumes the truth of the postulate expounded by some philosophical theories that words and concepts have no referential value. Alternative E presents a farfetched ethical judgment whose plausibility rests on the assumption that social groups are secretive and that the function of language is to exclude communication beyond the social group.

Question-type IX
As in the previous section the questions in this section measure the ability to solve a problem when all the facts relevant to its solution are not given. More specifically, many jobs require the employee to discover connections between events sometimes apparently unrelated. In order to do this the employee will find it necessary to correctly infer that unspecified events have probably occurred or are likely to occur. This ability becomes especially important when action must be taken on incomplete information. Accordingly, these questions

require competitors to choose among five suggested alternatives, each of which presents a different sequential arrangement of five events. Competitors must choose the MOST logical of the five suggested sequences. In order to do so, they MAY be required to draw on general knowledge to infer missing concepts or events that are essential to sequencing the five given events. Competitors should be careful to infer only what is essential to the sequence. The plausibility of the wrong alternatives will always require the inclusion of unlikely events or of additional chains of events which are NOT essential to sequencing the five given events.

1. 1. a body was found in the woods
    2. a man proclaimed innocence
    3. the owner of a gun was located
    4. a gun was traced
    5. the owner of a gun was questioned
        A) 4-3-5-2-1   D) 1-3-5-2-4
        B) 2-1-4-3-5   E) 1-2-4-3-5
        C) 1-4-3-5-2

The correct alternative, C, interrelates the events in the simplest and most logical sequence: if a body is found (1), it is probable that a weapon will be found and traced (4), that its owner will then be located (3) and questioned (5) and that he will proclaim his innocence (2). The plausibility of alternatives A and B rests on a more involved and less logical sequence because it requires the inclusion of an additional chain of events in order to make the discovery of a body (1) follow from a proclamation of innocence (2). The plausibility of alternative D likewise requires the inclusion of an additional chain of events to explain why a man would be located and questioned before the gun was traced. Sequence E rests on the assumption that the owner of the gun and the man proclaiming innocence are two persons. In this case the man proclaiming innocence loses his relation to the other events and becomes superfluous unless additional events are included.

2. 1. a man was in a hunting accident
    2. a man fell down a flight of steps
    3. a man lost his vision in one eye
    4. a man broke his leg
    5. a man had to walk with a cane
        A) 2-4-5-1-3   D) 1-3-5-2-4
        B) 4-5-1-3-2   E) 1-3-2-4-5
        C) 3-1-4-5-2

The correct alternative, E, provides the most likely causal relationship for the five events. Accidents with weapons such as those used when hunting (1) can result in a loss of vision (3). One-eyed vision impedes depth perception and could result in a fall down a flight of steps (2) causing a broken leg (4) and necessitating the use of a cane (5). Alternatives A and B are less plausible because they establish a causal rela-

tionship between walking with a cane and having the type of hunting accident that results in loss of vision. In addition, it is less likely that a man with a broken leg would go hunting than that a man with impaired vision would have to go up or down steps. Alternative D is less plausible than E because a broken leg rather than impaired vision is likely to necessitate the use of a cane. Alternative C is less plausible than E because it is likely that a loss of vision will follow rather than precede a hunting accident. Also, a broken leg is more likely to result from a fall than from a hunting accident.

3. 1. a man is offered a new job
    2. a woman is offered a new job
    3. a man works as a waiter
    4. a woman works as a waitress
    5. a woman gives notice
        A) 4-2-5-3-1   D) 3-1-4-2-5
        B) 4-2-5-1-3   E) 4-3-2-5-1
        C) 2-4-5-3-1

The correct alternative, B, provides the best temporal sequence for the five events by establishing a causal relationship where the three events concerning the woman trigger the two events concerning the man. A woman works as a waitress (4); she is offered a new job (2); gives notice to her employer (5); who offers her job to a man (1); who begins work as a waiter (3) when the woman leaves. The other four alternatives describe plausible situations but do not establish a causal relationship between the two sets of events. Thus if the new job that is offered to the man is not the one vacated by the woman, there is no way to determine whether a woman works as a waitress (4) before a man works as a waiter (3) or vice versa unless additional events are included.

4. 1. a train left the station late
    2. a man was late for work
    3. a man lost his job
    4. many people complained because the train was late
    5. there was a traffic jam
        A) 5-2-1-4-3   D) 1-5-4-2-3
        B) 5-1-4-2-3   E) 2-1-4-5-3
        C) 5-1-2-4-3

The correct alternative, A, follows from the inference that the man who is late for work is essential to the departure of the train. This is the only assumption that leads to a logical and interrelated sequence for the five events. The other four alternatives do not really interrelate the events and become plausible only if numerous assumptions are made. In addition, the four alternatives sever the connection between the numerous complaints (4) and the lost job (3). Without this connection event 4 becomes superfluous.

11

EXAMINATION SECTION

TEST 1

DIRECTIONS: Each question or incomplete statement is followed by several suggested answers or completions. Select the one that BEST answers the question or completes the statement. *PRINT THE CORRECT ANSWER IN THE SPACE AT THE RIGHT.*

1. To learn a foreign LANGGWAYJ is tedious work.
   The word in capitals is misspelled. Write it correctly at the right.

   1.___

2. The APRENTIS learns a trade.
   The word in capitals is misspelled. Write it correctly at the right.

   2.___

3. The SOHRS of the stream is high in the hills.
   The word in capitals is misspelled. Write it correctly at the right.

   3.___

4. Animals often show great INTELIJENS.
   The word in capitals is misspelled. Write it correctly at the right.

   4.___

5. Our hotels AKOMODAYT many people.
   The word in capitals is misspelled. Write it correctly at the right.

   5.___

6. Who determines whether a Congressman who is considered undesirable shall be seated?
   A. Congress   B. Supreme Court   C. President
   D. Cabinet   E. The people

   6.___

7. *Aviation in the United States is accomplishing much. The total number of miles flown annually now amounts to more than the total for any other country in the world and is about equal to the combined mileage of Germany and France.*
   According to the above paragraph, which one of the following statements is TRUE?
   A. The total number of miles flown annually in the United States is less than that of any other country.
   B. Germany leads in the number of miles flown annually.
   C. The United States surpasses every country in the world in the number of miles flown annually.
   D. Both Germany and France have greater air mileage than the United States.
   E. Because of the bigger size of the United States, our planes must fly farther than the planes in the rest of the countries combined.

   7.___

8. DIG is to TRENCH as BUILD is to   8._
   A. excavator   B. wall   C. mine
   D. construct   E. replace

9. TIGER is to CAT as WOLF is to   9._
   A. snarl B. dog   C. fur   D. wild   E. hunted

10. GENEROUS is to MISERLY as FRIENDLY is to   10._
   A. surly B. kind   C. stingy D. weak   E. clever

11. EAST is to WEST as DOWN is to   11._
   A. earth B. up   C. out   D. sky   E. rise

12. CLOTHES are to FABRIC as HOUSE is to   12._
   A. lot   B. shelter   C. wood
   D. residence   E. large

13. BOSTON is to SEASHORE as PITTSBURGH is to   13._
   A. capitol   B. inland   C. smaller
   D. city   E. agriculture

14. I wish to build a tank 5 feet long and 4 feet high that   14._
will hold 300 gallons.
What will the width of the tank be if 7½ gallons equal
1 cubic foot?

15. By what number is 3/4 of the product of 12 x 5 multiplied   15._
to give 405?

16. *Specimen signatures of consignee and consignor are sent*   16._
on form 6006.
What one word in the above sentence indicates the receiver?

17. CAUCASIAN is to WHITE MAN as MONGOLIAN is to   17._
   A. Black   B. Indian   C. Moor
   D. Chinese   E. mountaineers

18. *There is many a slip between the cup and the lip.*   18._
The above quotation means MOST NEARLY
   A. in life, as in wine, drink not to the dregs
   B. forget past troubles
   C. don't be too sure of the future
   D. a full cup spells prosperity
   E. a steady hand in all things is a necessity

19. *A new invention restores colors which were lost to some*   19._
talking motion pictures when the soundtrack was introduced
along the edge of the photographic film. By this new
development, a producer may 'turn on the moonlight' for
love scenes or use all the tints from blue to red in the
gamut of human emotions.
Judging from the above paragraph, which one of the following statements is TRUE?
   A. Colors cannot be used with the talkies.
   B. Only red or blue can be used in motion pictures.

C. A producer can now use all colors in talking films.
D. Human emotions can be shown only with moonlight pictures.

20. LAUGHTER is to REJOICING as WEEPING is to   20.___
    A. punishment   B. parting   C. sorrow
    D. disappointment   E. disillusionment

21. IRON is to HEAVY as FEATHERS are to   21.___
    A. goose   B. gray   C. light   D. grown   E. metal

22. AGREE is the opposite of   22.___
    A. quarrel   B. deny   C. warn
    D. dislike   E. unpleasant

23. ABUNDANT is the opposite of   23.___
    A. plenty   B. bouncing   C. scarce
    D. low   E. rare

24. He played the part of the VILIN.   24.___
    The word in capitals is misspelled. Write it correctly
    at the right.

25. These parts are INTURCHAYNJUBUL.   25.___
    The word in capitals is misspelled. Write it correctly
    at the right.

KEY (CORRECT ANSWERS)

1. language
2. apprentice
3. source
4. intelligence
5. accommodate

6. A
7. C
8. B
9. B
10. A

11. B
12. C
13. B
14. 2 ft.
15. 9

16. consignee
17. D
18. C
19. C
20. C

21. C
22. A
23. C
24. villain
25. interchangeable

TEST 2

DIRECTIONS: Each question or incomplete statement is followed by several suggested answers or completions. Select the one that BEST answers the question or completes the statement. *PRINT THE CORRECT ANSWER IN THE SPACE AT THE RIGHT.*

1. Extreme heat will LIKWIFY.
The word in capitals is misspelled. Write it correctly at the right.

1.____

2. It was his birthday ANIVURSAREE.
The word in capitals is misspelled. Write it correctly at the right.

2.____

3. The kittens were FROLIKING in the grass.
The word in capitals is misspelled. Write it correctly at the right.

3.____

4. C is to CC as AB is to
   A. ABC   B. AA   C. BB   D. AABB   E. AAB

4.____

5. RIVER is to AMAZON as LAKE is to
   A. deep   B. Ohio   C. Superior
   D. island   E. Mississippi

5.____

6. Which one of the following answers may be applied to LAKE MICHIGAN but not to LAKE ERIE and LAKE ONTARIO?
   A. Fresh water   B. Inland
   C. Navigable   D. St. Lawrence waterway
   E. Not adjacent to Canada

6.____

7. A tank can be filled through an intake pipe in 6 hours and emptied through an outlet pipe in 10 hours.
If the tank is empty and both intake and outlet pipes are opened, how long will it take the tank to fill?

7.____

8. A boy paid 36¢ for marbles. He lost three and then sold 1/3 of the remainder at cost for 9¢.
How many marbles did he buy originally?

8.____

9. *Whenever there are urgent reasons for filling a vacancy in any position in the competitive division and the director is unable to certify to the appointing officer, upon requisition by the latter, a list of persons eligible for appointment after a competitive examination, the appointing officer may nominate a person to the director for noncompetitive examination, and if such nominee is certified by the said director as qualified after such noncompetitive examination, he may be appointed provisionally to fill the vacancy only until a selection and appointment can be made after competitive examination, but no such appointment shall be continued for more than thirty days and successive appointments shall not be made.*

9.____

The above paragraph states that
   A. when no eligible register exists, appointments may
      be made to permanent positions by noncompetitive
      examinations of applicants
   B. appointment is made only of the person nominated by
      the appointing officer
   C. if an appointment continues for more than thirty days,
      it becomes permanent
   D. permanent appointment can be made only after success-
      ful competitive examination
   E. when an urgent need for filling a vacancy exists, it
      may be filled permanently without holding an examina-
      tion

10. PHASES means   10.____
    A. varying aspects   B. sentences
    C. frightening   D. bluffing
    E. receptacle for flowers

11. AUGMENT means MOST NEARLY   11.____
    A. forecast   B. increase   C. drill
    D. hollow out   E. sell

12. CYNICAL means MOST NEARLY   12.____
    A. cone shaped   B. faithless   C. morose
    D. sneering   E. cutting

13. ALLEGES means MOST NEARLY   13.____
    A. suspects   B. studies   C. claims
    D. fears   E. denies

14. ACCOSTED means MOST NEARLY   14.____
    A. reviled   B. hated   C. liked
    D. addressed   E. deceived

15. ABSOLVED means MOST NEARLY   15.____
    A. acquitted   B. responsible   C. anointed
    D. discovered   E. vain

16. ABANDON means MOST NEARLY   16.____
    A. enthusiasm   B. skill   C. loss
    D. unrestraint   E. listlessness

17. APPREHENSIVE means MOST NEARLY   17.____
    A. angry   B. guilty   C. anxious
    D. generous   E. arrested

18. Two-thirds of a hay crop was sold. One-half of the   18.____
    remainder was used for fodder and 60 bales still remained
    unused.
    How many bales were there in the entire crop?

19. A clerk threw off 1/3 of the mail sacks at A and 1/5 of the remainder at B. He then had 48 bags left. How many were on the train when he started?

19.___

20. A man's salary was increased by 25%. He was then earning $175 a month. What did he earn before the increase?

20.___

21. Street car tracks run PAIRULEL. The word in capitals is misspelled. Write it correctly at the right.

21.___

22. They went KANOOING on the river. The word in capitals is misspelled. Write it correctly at the right.

22.___

23. It is unwise to keep a VISHUS dog. The word in capitals is misspelled. Write it correctly at the right.

23.___

24. *That which comes through hard work is most appreciated.* The above quotation means MOST NEARLY
    A. easy riches lose their value
    B. easy come, easy go
    C. we appreciate that most which is hard to get
    D. hard work brings success

24.___

25. ALERTNESS is to SUCCESS as PROCRASTINATION is to
    A. idleness   B. failure   C. postponement
    D. leisure   E. uselessness

25.___

KEY (CORRECT ANSWERS)

1. liquefy	11. B
2. anniversary	12. D
3. frolicking	13. C
4. D	14. D
5. C	15. A
6. E	16. D
7. 15	17. C
8. 12	18. 360
9. D	19. 90
10. A	20. $140

21. parallel
22. canoeing
23. vicious
24. C
25. B

TEST 3

DIRECTIONS: Each question or incomplete statement is followed by several suggested answers or completions. Select the one that BEST answers the question or completes the statement. *PRINT THE CORRECT ANSWER IN THE SPACE AT THE RIGHT.*

1. A raise in pay allowed for this month and including the   1.____
    previous month is called
       A. delayed   B. postponed   C. revertible
       D. retroactive   E. past due

2. Which one of the following applies to LOCK and MAILBOX   2.____
    but not to STAMP?
       A. Canceled   B. Soiled
       C. Government property   D. Metal
       E. Gummed

3. INTEREST ON LOANS is to TIME as PARCEL POST RATES are to   3.____
       A. notes   B. weight   C. amount
       D. yearly   E. distance

4. To ATTEST is to   4.____
       A. heed   B. bear witness   C. make an oath
       D. try   E. question

5. F.O.B. is to FREIGHT SHIPMENT as C.O.D. is to   5.____
       A. charge account   B. store sales
       C. customers   D. package delivery
       E. purchases

6. *Blessed is he who has found his work.*   6.____
    The above quotation means MOST NEARLY
       A. despatch is the soul of business
       B. thrice happy they who have an occupation
       C. drive your business, let not it drive you
       D. business neglected is business lost
       E. unoccupied is unprofitable

7. *The empty vessel makes the greatest sound.*   7.____
    The above quotation means MOST NEARLY
       A. the dog that means to bite doesn't bark
       B. a boaster and a liar are cousins
       C. a deep stream flows silently
       D. aim above the mark to hit the mark
       E. the failure tells everyone how to run his business

8. *Hitch your wagon to a star.*   8.____
    The above quotation means MOST NEARLY
       A. a bird in the hand is worth two in the bush
       B. aim high and you will hit high
       C. as good do nothing as to no purpose
       D. your ability should determine your aim
       E. let nothing stop you

9. *Little things are great to little men.*
The above quotation means MOST NEARLY
   A. the elephant does not feel the flea bite
   B. little leaks sink great ships
   C. small minds are won by trifles
   D. drop by drop the tank is drained
   E. big oaks from little acorns grow

9.__

10. *A pound of pluck is worth a ton of luck.*
The above quotation means MOST NEARLY
   A. lucky men are as rare as white crows
   B. good luck is often bad luck
   C. diligence is the mother of good luck
   D. luck may carry a man across the brook if he will but leap
   E. courage overcomes more than luck

10.__

11. To DISTRIBUTE is to
   A. agitate   B. collect   C. dispense
   D. derange   E. disintegrate

11.__

12. A REMARKABLE occurrence is
   A. commonplace   B. extraordinary   C. needful
   D. uneventful   E. portentous

12.__

13. WHALE is to LARGE as THUNDER is to
   A. lightning   B. injure   C. rain
   D. loud   E. distant

13.__

14. *If you are shipping canned goods from Wisconsin to San Francisco, the goods can be put down in the San Francisco market cheaper if they are hauled east by train and then carried all the way around the coast by water. For the interstate commerce commission has so built its rate structure that it is cheaper for the Wisconsin farmer to go 4,000 miles out of his way than use the direct rail route west.*
According to the above paragraph, which one of the following statements is TRUE?
   A. The Wisconsin farmer must go 4,000 miles out of his way to ship goods to the west coast.
   B. To ship the goods by water will save time.
   C. He can save money by shipping by the direct rail route west.
   D. In sending goods to the west coast, it is cheaper for him to send them 6,000 miles by water and rail than 2,000 miles by rail only

14.__

15. *The Atlantic Ocean is noted for the Gulf Stream which passes northward from the Gulf of Mexico, but which preserves its warmth until it reaches the British Isles. This is one of the reasons why England enjoys a warmer climate than Labrador, though both are in about the same latitude. The countries of southern Europe gain much of their warmth from the winds that blow across the Mediterranean Sea from the Sahara Desert.*

15.__

According to the above paragraph, which one of the follow-
ing statements is TRUE?
England is warmer than Labrador because
  A. the warm winds from the Sahara Desert reach England
  B. England is farther south than Labrador
  C. the Gulf Stream becomes cold before it reaches
    Labrador
  D. the Gulf Stream stays warm until it reaches England
  E. the Gulf of Mexico is directly across the ocean
    from England

16. *On the west coast, a campaign for a safe and sane Fourth*   16.___
*of July was started, resulting in laws that forbade the
sale of fireworks in that section. The Fourth there is
one of the quietest days of the year, the people expressing their patriotism in less harmful, though equally
enjoyable, ways. In the east, where tradition is strong,
there is no such law; but a tradition that brings in its
wake the many tragedies that fireworks do is more honored
in the breach than in the observance.*
According to the above paragraph, which one of the following statements is TRUE?
The use of fireworks on the Fourth of July
  A. has been forbidden in all eastern states
  B. is traditional and so should not be prohibited
  C. is the only enjoyable way in which patriotism can be
    expressed
  D. is forbidden in certain western states
  E. causes very few accidents

17. A man was 69 years old on October 20th, 1992. Through 1992,   17.___
in how many presidential elections could he have voted?

18. Two mechanics were repairing a motor, and one of the men,   18.___
without knowing it, rubbed a smudge of grease on his face.
When the job was completed, they looked at each other and
the man with the clean face washed his face while the one
with the dirty face did not.
Which one of the following statements will explain this
action?
  A. The man with the clean face wanted to impress his
    employer.
  B. They always washed their faces after completing a job.
  C. The man with the clean face thought his own face
    might be dirty.
  D. The man with the dirty face did not care about his
    appearance.
  E. The man with the dirty face was about to start
    another job.

19. *In withdrawing stamps, postal cards, stamped envelopes,*   19.___
*and newspaper wrappers from the reserve stock, postmaster
should select the oldest on hand for sale to the public,
provided they are in perfect condition. This will lessen
the chances for stock to become shopworn and damaged, and*

tend to keep it fresh. Damaged or soiled stamped paper or stamps should never be offered for sale to the public.
According to the above paragraph, which one of the following statements is TRUE?
- A. Postmasters should offer for sale only new, fresh stocks of stamps.
- B. All old stock, regardless of condition, should be quickly sold.
- C. Oldest stock, in perfect condition, should be sold first.
- D. All old stock of stamps should be withdrawn and not offered for sale.
- E. Imperfect stamps should be sold quickly before they become old.

20. *At the time of his Gettysburg Address, Lincoln himself had no knowledge of what the final result of the Civil War was to be. He knew that the great principles for which he had stood were the principles on which the war was being fought. He knew that his own firm resolution and deep patriotism had sent thousands to their deaths and that many thousands more might die. With his mind burdened with unthinkable responsibilities, he took his place on the still scarred battlefield and spoke not only to soldiers, but to the fathers and mothers of boys who might that very day be meeting death in distant battlefields.*
Judging entirely from the above quotation, which one of the following statements is TRUE?
- A. The Battle of Gettysburg was in progress when Lincoln made this Address.
- B. Lincoln's patriotic principles were the underlying cause of the war.
- C. Lincoln was in sympathy with the principles on which the war was being fought.
- D. The Civil War had come to a close when Lincoln made his Gettysburg Address.
- E. The fathers and mothers of the soldiers were present at the Battle of Gettysburg.

20. _____

KEY (CORRECT ANSWERS)

1.	D	11.	C
2.	D	12.	B
3.	E	13.	D
4.	B	14.	D
5.	D	15.	D
6.	B	16.	D
7.	E	17.	13
8.	B	18.	C
9.	C	19.	C
10.	E	20.	C

GENERAL AND MENTAL ABILITY

COMMENTARY

No matter what the level of the examination tested for, be it for trainee or administrator, whether a specific substantive examination is drawn up *ad hoc* for the position announced or whether a brief, simple qualifying test is given, keen analysis of current testing practices reveals that the type of question indicative of general or mental ability or aptitude, or *intelligence*, is an inevitable component and/or element of most examinations.

In other words, the examiners assume that all candidates must possess, or show, a certain level of understanding or *good sense* in matters or situations that may be considered common or general to all. This, then, is the purpose of the general-or-mental-type question: it seems to delimn, in objective terms, the basic, clearly definable, mental or intellectual status of the examinee, no matter what his education or his training or his experience or his present position or reputation.

In some cases, and for certain whole fields of job positions, tests of general and mental ability have even supplanted the specialized subject-area or position-information examination.

Moreover, even in the latter type of examination, e.g., the specific position-type, it will be found that questions testing general qualities study the examination at point after point.

This section should be of inestimable value to the candidate as he prepares not only for the job-examination, but also for any other examination that he may take at this time or in the future.

Now the candidate should *take* the tests of general and mental ability that follow, because of this special importance. These, particularly, portray the extended and rounded examination of general and/or mental ability.

The *Tests* that follow also serve to focus the candidate's attention on the variety and types of questions to be encountered, and to familiarize him with answer-patterns-and-nuances.

———

EXAMINATION SECTION
TEST 1

DIRECTIONS: Each question or incomplete statement is followed by several suggested answers or completions. Select the one that BEST answers the question or completes the statement. *PRINT THE CORRECT ANSWER IN THE SPACE AT THE RIGHT.*

1. The OPPOSITE of defeat is   1.___
   A. glory   B. honor   C. victory
   D. success   E. hope

2. If 3 pencils cost 10 cents, how many pencils can be bought   2.___
   for 50 cents?

3. A dog does NOT always have   3.___
   A. eyes   B. bones   C. a nose
   D. a collar   E. lungs

4. The OPPOSITE of strange is   4.___
   A. peculiar   B. familiar   C. unusual
   D. quaint   E. extraordinary

5. A lion MOST resembles a   5.___
   A. dog   B. goat   C. cat   D. cow   E. horse

6. Sound is related to quiet in the same way that sunlight   6.___
   is to
   A. darkness   B. evaporation   C. bright
   D. a cellar   E. noise

7. A party consisted of a man and his wife, his three sons   7.___
   and their wives, and two children in each son's family.
   How many were there in the party?

8. A man ALWAYS has   8.___
   A. children   B. nerves   C. teeth
   D. home   E. wife

9. The OPPOSITE of stingy is   9.___
   A. wealthy   B. extravagant   C. poor
   D. economical   E. generous

10. Lead is cheaper than silver because it is   10.___
    A. duller   B. more plentiful   C. softer
    D. uglier   E. less useful

Questions 11-13.

DIRECTIONS: Answer Questions 11 through 13 by choosing the CORRECT proverb meaning given below.

     A. Eat heartily at a good feast.
     B. Only exceptional misfortunes harm all concerned.

C. Don't invite trouble by stirring it up.
D. Strong winds blow harder than weak ones.
E. Too much of anything is no better than a sufficiency.
F. Tired dogs need lots of sleep.

11. Which statement above explains the proverb, *Let sleeping dogs lie*?   11.__

12. Which statement above explains the proverb, *Enough is as good as a feast*?   12.__

13. Which statement above explains the proverb, *It's an ill wind that blows nobody good*?   13.__

14. A radio is related to a telephone as _____ is to a railroad train.   14.__
    A. a highway   B. an airplane   C. gasoline
    D. speed   E. noise

15. If a boy can run at the rate of 8 feet in 1/3 of a second, how far can he run in 10 seconds? 240 1720   15.__

16. A debate ALWAYS involves   16.__
    A. an audience   B. judges   C. a prize
    D. a controversy   E. an auditorium

17. Of the five words below, four are alike in a certain way. Which one is NOT like these four?   17.__
    A. Walk   B. Run   C. Kneel   D. Skip   E. Jump

18. The OPPOSITE of frequently is   18.__
    A. seldom   B. occasionally   C. never
    D. sometimes   E. often

19. A thermometer is related to temperature as a speedometer is to   19.__
    A. fast   B. automobile   C. velocity
    D. time   E. heat

20. Which word makes the TRUEST sentence?   20.__
Women are _____ shorter than their husbands.
    A. always   B. usually   C. much
    D. rarely   E. never

21. 1 6 2 7 3 8 4 9 5 10 7 11   21.__
One number is wrong in the above series.
What should that number be? 6

22. All children in this class are good students.   22.__
John is not a good student.
John is a member of this class.
If the first two statements are true, the third is
    A. true   B. false   C. not certain

23. A boat race ALWAYS has   23.___
    A. oars   B. spectators   C. victory
    D. contestants   E. sails

24.   4 2 3 1 5 6 8 7 3 4 6 6 4 3 2 5 1 8 6 7 9   24.___
Which number in this row appears a second time nearest
the beginning?

25. The sun is related to the earth as the earth is to   25.___
    A. clouds   B. rotation   C. the universe
    D. the moon   E. circumference

———

KEY (CORRECT ANSWERS)

1. C		11. C
2. 15		12. E
3. D		13. B
4. B		14. B
5. C		15. 240
6. A		16. D
7. 14		17. C
8. B		18. A
9. E		19. C
10. B		20. B

21. 6
22. B
23. D
24. 3
25. D

———

TEST 2

DIRECTIONS: Each question or incomplete statement is followed by
several suggested answers or completions. Select the
one that BEST answers the question or completes the
statement. *PRINT THE CORRECT ANSWER IN THE SPACE AT
THE RIGHT.*

1. Which word makes the TRUEST sentence?   1.__
    A youth is _____ wiser than his father.
       A. never   B. rarely   C. much
       D. usually   E. always

2. The OPPOSITE of graceful is   2.__
       A. weak   B. ugly   C. slow
       D. awkward   E. uncanny

3. A grandmother is always _____ than her granddaughter.   3.__
       A. smarter   B. more quiet   C. older
       D. smaller   E. slower

Questions 4-6.

DIRECTIONS: Answer Questions 4 through 6 by choosing the CORRECT
proverb meaning given below.

    A. Even the darkest situations have their bright aspects.
    B. The final result is more important than the intermediate steps
    C. Handsome persons always do pleasing things.
    D. All comes out well in the end.
    E. Persons whose actions please us seem good-looking.
    F. Clouds shimmer as if they were made of silver.

4. Which statement above explains the proverb, *All's well*   4.__
    that ends well?

5. Which statement above explains the proverb, *Every cloud*   5.__
    has a silver lining?

6. Which statement above explains the proverb, *Handsome is*   6.__
    that handsome does?

7. If the settlement of a difference between two parties is   7.__
    made by a third party, it is called a(n)
       A. compromise   B. truce   C. promise
       D. injunction   E. arbitration

8. Oil is to toil as _____ is to hate.   8.__
       A. love   B. work   C. boil   D. ate   E. hat

9. Of the five words below, four are alike in a certain way.   9.___
   Which one is NOT like these four?
      A. Push   B. Hold   C. Lift   D. Drag   E. Pull

10. If 10 boxes full of apples weigh 300 pounds and each box   10.___
    when empty weighs 3 pounds, how many pounds do all the
    apples weigh?

11. The OPPOSITE of sorrow is   11.___
       A. fun   B. success   C. hope
       D. prosperity   E. joy

12. A B C D E F G H I J K L M N O P Q R S T U V W X Y Z   12.___
    If all the odd-numbered letters in the alphabet were
    crossed out, what would be the twelfth letter NOT
    crossed out?

13. What letter in the word *unfortunately* is the same number   13.___
    in the word (counting from the beginning) as it is in
    the alphabet?

14. Such traits as honesty, sincerity, and loyalty constitute   14.___
    one's
       A. personality   B. reputation   C. wisdom
       D. character   E. success

15. If 3 1/3 yards of cloth cost 25 cents, what will 10 yards   15.___
    cost?

16. same   means   small   little   the   as   16.___
    If the above words were arranged to make a good sentence,
    with what letter would the second word of the sentence
    begin? (Make it like a printed capital.)

17. George is younger than Frank.   17.___
    James is younger than George.
    Frank is older than James.
    If the first two statements are true, the third is
       A. true   B. false   C. not certain

18. Suppose that the first and second letters in the word   18.___
    abolitionist were interchanged, also the third and fourth
    letters, the fifth and sixth, etc.
    Print the letter that would be the tenth letter counting
    to the right.

19. 0 1 3 6 10 15 21 29 36   19.___
    One number is wrong in the above series.
    What should that number be?

20. If 3½ yards of cloth cost 70 cents, what will 4½ yards   20.___
    cost?

21. A person who never pretends to be anything other than
    what he is, is said to be
       A. loyal   B. hypocritical   C. sincere
       D. meek   E. courageous

                                                         21.___

22. Which of these words is related to many as exceptional
    is to ordinary?
       A. None   B. Each   C. More   D. Much   E. Few

                                                           22.___

23. The OPPOSITE of cowardly is
       A. brave   B. strong   C. treacherous
       D. loyal   E. friendly

                                                           23.___

24. Which one of the five words below is MOST unlike the
    other four?
       A. Fast   B. Agile   C. Quick   D. Run   E. Speedy

                                                           24.___

25. Some of Brown's friends are Catholics.
    Some of Brown's friends are lawyers.
    Some of Brown's friends are Catholic lawyers.
    If the first two statements are true, the third is
       A. true   B. false   C. not certain

                                                           25.___

KEY (CORRECT ANSWERS)

1. B		11. E
2. D		12. X
3. C		13. L
4. B		14. D
5. A		15. 75
6. E		16. M
7. E		17. A
8. D		18. N
9. B		19. 28
10. 270		20. 90

                         21. C
                         22. E
                         23. A
                         24. D
                         25. C

TEST 3

DIRECTIONS: Each question or incomplete statement is followed by several suggested answers or completions. Select the one that BEST answers the question or completes the statement. *PRINT THE CORRECT ANSWER IN THE SPACE AT THE RIGHT.*

1. How many of the following words can be made from the letters in the word *strangle*, using any letter any number of times: greatest, tangle, garage, stresses, related, grease, nearest, reeling?

    1.___

2. To insist that trees can talk to one another is
    A. absurd   B. misleading   C. improbable
    D. unfair   E. wicked

    2.___

3. Of the things following, four are alike in a certain way. Which one is NOT like these four?
    A. Snow   B. Soot   C. Cotton   D. Ivory   E. Milk

    3.___

4. A square is related to a circle in the same way in which a pyramid is related to
    A. a solid   B. Egypt   C. height
    D. a cone   E. a circumference

    4.___

5. If the following words were seen on a wall by looking in a mirror on the opposite wall, which word would appear exactly the same as if seen directly?
    A. Meet   B. Rotor   C. Mama   D. Deed   E. Toot

    5.___

6. If a strip of cloth 32 inches long will shrink to 28 inches when washed, how many inches long will a 24-inch strip of the same cloth be after shrinking?

    6.___

7. Which of the following is a trait of character?
    A. Ability   B. Reputation   C. Hate
    D. Stinginess   E. Nervousness

    7.___

8. Find the two letters in the word *coming* which have just as many letters between them in the word as in the alphabet. Print the one of these letters that comes FIRST in the alphabet.

    8.___

9. Modern is to ancient as _____ is to yesterday.
    A. tomorrow   B. time   C. up-to-date
    D. history   E. today

    9.___

10. 1 2 4 8 16 32 64 96
    One number is wrong in the above series.
    What should that number be?

    10.___

11. If George can ride a bicycle 40 feet while Frank runs   11.__
    30 feet, how far can George ride while Frank runs 45 feet?

12. L U L R V E L U R E U L U U L V E L L U V L U R U L O   12.__
    E V L U E
    Count each L in this series that is followed by a U next
    to it if the U is not followed by an R next to it.
    Tell how many L's you count.

13. A man who is in favor of marked change is said to be   13.__
       A. democratic   B. conservative   C. radical
       D. anarchistic   E. republican

14. Print the letter which is the fourth letter to the left   14.__
    of the letter midway between N and R in the alphabet.

Questions 15-17.

DIRECTIONS: Questions 15 through 17 are to be answered on the
               basis of the following figure.

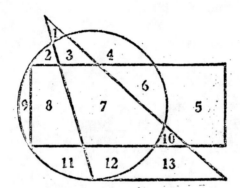

15. What number is in the space which is in the rectangle   15.__
    but not in the triangle or in the circle?

16. What number is in the same geometrical figure or figures   16.__
    (and no other) as the number 3?

17. How many spaces are there that are in any one but only   17.__
    one geometrical figure?

18. A line is related to a surface as a point is to a   18.__
       A. circle   B. line   C. solid
       D. dot   E. intersection

19. One cannot become a good lawyer without diligent study.   19.__
    George studies law diligently.
    George will become a good lawyer.
    If the first two statements are true, the third is
       A. true   B. false   C. not certain

20. honesty traits Generosity character of desirable   20.___
    and are
    If the above words are arranged to make the BEST sentence,
    with what letter will the last word of the sentence end?
    (Print the letter as a capital.)

21. A man who carefully considers all available information   21.___
    before making a decision is said to be
         A. influential   B. prejudiced   C. decisive
         D. hypocritical   E. impartial

22. A hotel serves a mixture of 2 parts cream and 3 parts milk.   22.___
    How many pints of milk will it take to make 25 pints of
    the mixture?

23. _____ is related to stars as physiology is to blood.   23.___
         A. Telescope   B. Darkness   C. Astronomy
         D. Light waves   E. Chemistry

24. A statement based upon a supposition is said to be   24.___
         A. erroneous   B. ambiguous   C. distorted
         D. hypothetical   E. doubtful

25. If a wire 40 inches long is to be cut so that one piece   25.___
    is 2/3 as long as the other piece, how many inches long
    must the shorter piece be?

KEY (CORRECT ANSWERS)

1. 6		11. 60	
2. A		12. 4	
3. B		13. C	
4. D		14. L	
5. E		15. 5	
6. 21		16. 12	
7. D		17. 7	
8. G		18. B	
9. E		19. C	
10. 128		20. R	

             21. E
             22. 15
             23. C
             24. D
             25. 16

EXAMINATION SECTION

DIRECTIONS: Each question or incomplete statement is followed by several suggested answers or completions. Select the one that BEST answers the question or completes the statement. *PRINT THE LETTER OF THE CORRECT ANSWER IN THE SPACE AT THE RIGHT.*

Questions 1-10.

DIRECTIONS: Select the alternative that means the *same as* or the *opposite* of the word in italics.

1. *acquire*
   A. judge   B. identify   C. surrender
   D. educate   E. happen   1.____

2. *begrudge*
   A. envy   B. hate   C. annoy
   D. obstruct   E. punish   2.____

3. *obsolete*
   A. fatal   B. modern   C. distracting
   D. untouched   E. broken   3.____

4. *inflexible*
   A. weak   B. righteous   C. harmless
   D. unyielding   E. secret   4.____

5. *nominal*
   A. just   B. slight   C. cheerful
   D. familiar   E. ceaseless   5.____

6. *debt*
   A. insane   B. artificial   C. skillful
   D. determined   E. humble   6.____

7. *censure*
   A. focus   B. exclude   C. baffle
   D. portray   E. praise   7.____

8. *nebulous*
   A. imaginary   B. spiritual   C. distinct
   D. starry-eyed   E. unanswerable   8.____

9. *impart*
   A. hasten   B. adjust   C. gamble
   D. address   E. communicate   9.____

10. *terminate*
    A. gain   B. graduate   C. harvest
    D. start   E. paralyze   10.____

Questions 11-20.

DIRECTIONS: Select the word which, if inserted in the blank space, agrees *most closely* with the thought of the sentence.

11. Every good story is carefully contrived; the elements of the story are ____ to fit with one another in order to make an effect on the reader.
    A. read   B. learned   C. emphasized
    D. reduced   E. planned

11.__

12. Their work was commemorative in character and consisted largely of ____ erected upon the occasion of victories.
    A. towers   B. tombs   C. monuments
    D. castles   E. fortresses

12.__

13. Before criticizing the work of an artist, one needs to ____ the artist's purpose.
    A. understand   B. reveal   C. defend
    D. correct   E. change

13.__

14. Because in the administration it hath respect not to the group but to the ____, our form of government is called a democracy.
    A. courts   B. people   C. majority
    D. individual   E. law

14.__

15. Deductive reasoning is that form of reasoning in which the conclusion must necessarily follow if we accept the premise as true. In deduction, it is ____ for the premise to be true and the conclusion false.
    A. impossible   B. inevitable   C. reasonable
    D. surprising   E. unlikely

15.__

16. Mathematics is the product of thought operating by means of ____ for the purpose of expressing general laws.
    A. reasoning   B. symbols   C. words
    D. examples   E. science

16.__

17. No other man loses so much, so ____, so absolutely, as the beaten candidate for high public office.
    A. bewilderingly   B. predictably   C. disgracefully
    D. publicly   E. cheerfully

17.__

18. Many television watchers enjoy stories which contain violence. Consequently, those television producers who are dominated by rating systems aim to ____ the popular taste.
    A. raise   B. control   C. gratify
    D. ignore   E. lower

18.__

19. The latent period for the contractile response to direct stimulation of the muscle has quite another and shorter value, encompassing only a utilization period. Hence, it is that the term *latent period* must be ____ carefully each time that it is used.
    A. checked   B. timed   C. introduced
    D. defined   E. selected

19.__

20. A man who cannot win honor in his own ____ will have a   20.___
    very small chance of winning it from posterity.
    A. right   B. field   C. country   D. way   E. age

Questions 21-35.

DIRECTIONS: Select the word that BEST completes the analogy.

21. Albino is to color as traitor is to   21.___
    A. patriotism   B. treachery   C. socialism
    D. integration   E. liberalism

22. Senile is to infantile as supper is to   22.___
    A. snack   B. breakfast   C. dinner
    D. daytime   E. evening

23. Snow shovel is to sidewalk as eraser is to   23.___
    A. writing   B. pencil   C. paper
    D. desk   E. mistake

24. Lawyer is to court as soldier is to   24.___
    A. battle   B. victory   C. training
    D. rifle   E. discipline

25. Faucet is to water as mosquito is to   25.___
    A. swamp   B. butterfly   C. cistern
    D. pond   E. malaria

26. Astronomy is to geology as steeplejack is to   26.___
    A. mailman   B. surgeon   C. pilot
    D. miner   E. skindiver

27. Chimney is to smoke as guide is to   27.___
    A. snare   B. compass   C. hunter
    D. firewood   E. wild game

28. Prodigy is to ability as ocean is to   28.___
    A. water   B. waves   C. ships
    D. icebergs   E. current

29. War is to devastation as microbe is to   29.___
    A. peace   B. flea   C. dog
    D. germ   E. pestilence

30. Blueberry is to pea as sky is to   30.___
    A. storm   B. world   C. star   D. grass   E. purity

31. Pour is to spill as lie is to   31.___
    A. deception   B. misstatement   C. falsehood
    D. perjury   E. fraud

32. Disparage is to despise as praise is to   32.___
    A. dislike   B. adore   C. acclaim
    D. advocate   E. compliment

33. Wall is to mortar as nation is to   33. ___
   A. family   B. people   C. patriotism
   D. geography   E. boundaries

34. Servant is to butler as pain is to   34. ___
   A. cramp   B. hurt   C. illness
   D. itch   E. anesthesia

35. Fan is to air as newspaper is to   35. ___
   A. literature   B. reporter   C. information
   D. subscription E. reader

Questions 36-45.

DIRECTIONS: Select the *alternative* that BEST answers the question.

36. A set of papers is arranged and numbered from 1 to 49.   36. ___
   If the paper numbered 3 is drawn first and every ninth
   paper thereafter, what will be the number of the last
   paper drawn?
   A. 45   B. 46   C. 47   D. 48   E. 49

37. Which quantity can be measured *exactly* from a tank of   37. ___
   water by using only a 10-pint can and an 8-pint can?
   ___ pint(s).
   A. 1   B. 6   C. 3   D. 7   E. 5

38. If city R has more fires than city S, and city T has more   38. ___
   fires than cities P and S combined, then the number of
   fires in city
   A. P must be less than in city T
   B. T must be less than in city R
   C. T must be greater than in city R
   D. R must be greater than in city P
   E. S must be greater than in city T

39. The average of three numbers is 25.   39. ___
   If one of the numbers is increased by 4, the average will
   remain unchanged if each of the other two numbers is
   reduced by
   A. 1   B. 2   C. 2/3   D. 4   E. 1 1/3

40. Below are the first six rows of a triangular array con-   40. ___
   structed according to a fixed law.
   What number does the letter X represent?

                         1
                       1   1
                     1   2   1
                   1   3   3   1
                 1   4   6   4   1
               1   5   10   X   5   1

   A. 8   B. 10   C. 15   D. 20   E. 5

41. If all A are C and no C are B, it necessarily follows that   41.____
   A. all B are C   B. all B are A   C. no A are B
   D. no C are A   E. some B are A

42. What number is missing in the series 7, ___, 63, 189?   42.____
   A. 9   B. 11   C. 19   D. 21   E. 24

43. A clock that gains one minute each hour is synchronized   43.____
   at noon with a clock that loses two minutes an hour.
   How many minutes apart will the minute hands of the two
   clocks be at midnight?
   A. 0   B. 12   C. 14   D. 24   E. 30

44. The pages of a typewritten report are numbered by hand   44.____
   from 1 to 100.
   How many times will it be necessary to write the numeral 5?
   A. 10   B. 11   C. 12   D. 19   E. 20

45. The number 6 is called a *perfect* number because it is   45.____
   the sum of all its integral divisors except itself.
   Another *perfect* number is
   A. 12   B. 16   C. 24   D. 28   E. 36

KEY (CORRECT ANSWERS)

1. C	11. E	21. A	31. B	41. C
2. A	12. C	22. B	32. B	42. D
3. B	13. A	23. C	33. C	43. D
4. D	14. D	24. A	34. A	44. E
5. B	15. A	25. E	35. C	45. D
6. C	16. B	26. D	36. D	
7. E	17. D	27. C	37. B	
8. C	18. C	28. A	38. A	
9. E	19. D	29. E	39. B	
10. D	20. E	30. D	40. B	

WORD MEANING
EXAMINATION SECTION
TEST 1

Questions 1-20.

DIRECTIONS: Each question consists of a statement. You are to indicate whether the statement is TRUE (T) or FALSE (F). *PRINT THE LETTER OF THE CORRECT ANSWER IN THE SPACE AT THE RIGHT.*

1. *To eliminate hand pumping means NEARLY the same as to do away with hand pumping.* 1.___

2. *Discarding a ladder with a cracked rung means NEARLY the same as repairing a ladder with a cracked rung.* 2.___

3. A *projecting* stub is USUALLY a stub which sticks out. 3.___

4. A *nitrogen deficiency* in the soil is an oversupply of nitrogen in the soil. 4.___

5. Saying that a soil has a heavy *texture* is NEARLY the same as saying that the soil has a deep color. 5.___

6. A *neutral* soil is one in which no useful plants will grow. 6.___

7. A plant which is *dormant* is USUALLY in an inactive period of growth. 7.___

8. Saying that sun is *detrimental* to ferns is NEARLY the same as saying that sun is harmful to ferns. 8.___

9. *Vendors are permitted only in certain park areas.* In this sentence, the word *vendors* means NEARLY the same as *sellers*. 9.___

10. *The Assistant Gardener was confident that he would be able to learn the new work quickly.* In this sentence, the word *confident* means NEARLY the same as *sure*. 10.___

11. *The employee's behavior on the job was improper.* In this sentence, the word *improper* means NEARLY the same as *good*. 11.___

12. *The foreman's oral instructions were always clear and to the point.* In this sentence, the word *oral* means NEARLY the same as *spoken*. 12.___

13. *A covering with paper will prevent excessive loss of moisture from the surface soil.* In this sentence, the word *excessive* means NEARLY the same as *unnecessary*. 13.___

14. *In making a permanent hotbed, the ground should be excavated to a depth of fifteen inches.* In this sentence, the word *excavated* means NEARLY the same as *dug out*. 14.___

15. *After the seed has been sown, an application of water will help it to germinate.* In this sentence, the word *germinate* means NEARLY the same as *start growing*.   15.___

16. *A sandy soil may be greatly improved through the incorporation of organic materials.* In this sentence, the word *incorporation* means NEARLY the same as *removal*.   16.___

17. *Manures are considered a concentrated form of fertilizer.* In this sentence, the word *concentrated* means NEARLY the same as *natural*.   17.___

18. *Ventilation of some kind must be given the plants.* In this sentence, the word *ventilation* means NEARLY the same as *heat*.   18.___

19. *When rain water enters soil, it penetrates air spaces.* In this sentence, the word *penetrates* means NEARLY the same as *fills*.   19.___

20. *The metal was corroded.* In this sentence, the word *corroded* means NEARLY the same as *polished*.   20.___

Questions 21-40.

DIRECTIONS: In answering Questions 21 through 40, select the lettered word which means MOST NEARLY the same as the capitalized word. *PRINT THE LETTER OF THE CORRECT ANSWER IN THE SPACE AT THE RIGHT.*

21. ACCURATE   21.___
    A. correct   B. useful   C. afraid   D. careless

22. ALTER   22.___
    A. copy   B. change   C. repeat   D. agree

23. DOCUMENT   23.___
    A. outline   B. agreement   C. blueprint   D. record

24. INDICATE   24.___
    A. listen   B. show   C. guess   D. try

25. INVENTORY   25.___
    A. custom   B. discovery   C. warning   D. list

26. ISSUE   26.___
    A. annoy   B. use up   C. give out   D. gain

27. NOTIFY   27.___
    A. inform   B. promise   C. approve   D. strengthen

28. ROUTINE   28.___
    A. path   B. mistake   C. habit   D. journey

2

29. TERMINATE   29.___
    A. rest   B. start   C. deny   D. end

30. TRANSMIT   30.___
    A. put in   B. send   C. stop   D. go across

31. QUARANTINE   31.___
    A. feed   B. keep separate
    C. clean   D. give an injection to

32. HERD   32.___
    A. group   B. pair   C. person   D. ear

33. SPECIES   33.___
    A. few   B. favorite   C. kind   D. small

34. INJURE   34.___
    A. hurt   B. need   C. protect   D. help

35. ANNOY   35.___
    A. like   B. answer   C. rest   D. bother

36. EXTINCT   36.___
    A. likely   B. no longer exists
    C. tired   D. gradually dying out

37. CONFINE   37.___
    A. fly about freely   B. free
    C. keep within limits   D. care

38. ENVIRONMENT   38.___
    A. distant   B. surroundings
    C. disease   D. lake

39. AVIARY   39.___
    A. pig pen   B. large bird cage
    C. elephant cage   D. snake pit

40. CRATE   40.___
    A. make   B. report   C. box   D. truck

3

TEST 2

Questions 1-6.

DIRECTIONS: Questions 1 through 6 are to be answered on the basis
of the following paragraph.

It is important that traffic signals be regularly and effective-ly maintained. Signals with impaired efficiency cannot be expected to command desired respect. Poorly maintained traffic signs create disrespect in the minds of those who are to obey them and thereby reduce the effectiveness and authority of the signs. Maintenance should receive paramount consideration in the design and purchase of traffic signal equipment. The initial step in a good maintenance program for traffic signals is the establishment of a maintenance record. This record should show the cost of operation and mainte-nance of different types of equipment. It should give complete information regarding signal operations and indicate where defective planning exists in maintenance programs.

1. The word *effectively*, as used in the above paragraph,   1.___
    means MOST NEARLY
    A. occasionally   B. properly
    C. expensively   D. cheaply

2. The word *impaired*, as used in the above paragraph, means   2.___
    MOST NEARLY
    A. reduced   B. increased C. constant   D. high

3. The word *desired*, as used in the above paragraph, means   3.___
    MOST NEARLY
    A. public   B. complete   C. wanted   D. enough

4. The word *paramount*, as used in the above paragraph, means   4.___
    MOST NEARLY
    A. little   B. chief   C. excessive D. some

5. The word *initial*, as used in the above paragraph, means   5.___
    MOST NEARLY
    A. first   B. final
    C. determining   D. most important

6. The word *defective*, as used in the above paragraph, means   6.___
    MOST NEARLY
    A. suitable B. real   C. good   D. faulty

Questions 7-31.

DIRECTIONS: Each of Questions 7 through 31 consists of a capitalized word followed by four suggested meanings of the word. For each question, choose the word or phrase which means MOST NEARLY the same as the capitalized word.

7. ABOLISH   7.___
  A. count up   B. do away with
  C. give more   D. pay double for

8. ABUSE   8.___
  A. accept B. mistreat C. respect D. touch

9. ACCURATE   9.___
  A. correct B. lost C. neat D. secret

10. ASSISTANCE   10.___
  A. attendance   B. belief
  C. help   D. reward

11. CAUTIOUS   11.___
  A. brave B. careful C. greedy D. hopeful

12. COURTEOUS   12.___
  A. better B. easy C. polite D. religious

13. CRITICIZE   13.___
  A. admit B. blame C. check on D. make dirty

14. DIFFICULT   14.___
  A. capable B. dangerous C. dull D. hard

15. ENCOURAGE   15.___
  A. aim at B. beg for C. cheer on D. free from

16. EXTENT   16.___
  A. age B. size C. truth D. wildness

17. EXTRAVAGANT   17.___
  A. empty B. helpful C. over D. wasteful

18. FALSE   18.___
  A. absent   B. colored
  C. not enough   D. wrong

19. INDICATE   19.___
  A. point out   B. show up
  C. shrink from   D. take to

20. NEGLECT   20.___
  A. disregard   B. flatten
  C. likeness   D. thoughtfulness

21. PENALIZE   21.__
    A. make   B. notice   C. pay   D. punish

22. POSTPONED   22.__
    A. put off   B. repeated   C. taught   D. went to

23. PUNCTUAL   23.__
    A. bursting   B. catching
    C. make a hole in   D. on time

24. RARE   24.__
    A. large   B. ride up   C. unusual   D. young

25. REVEAL   25.__
    A. leave   B. renew   C. soften   D. tell

26. EXCESSIVE   26.__
    A. excusable   B. immoderate
    C. ethereal   D. intentional

27. VOLUNTARY   27.__
    A. common   B. paid   C. sharing   D. willing

28. WHOLESOME   28.__
    A. cheap   B. healthful   C. hot   D. together

29. SERIOUS   29.__
    A. important   B. order   C. sharp   D. tight

30. TRIVIAL   30.__
    A. alive   B. empty   C. petty   D. troublesome

31. VENTILATE   31.__
    A. air out   B. darken
    C. last   D. take a chance

Questions 32-40.

DIRECTIONS: Each question consists of a statement. You are to
              indicate whether the statement is TRUE (T) or FALSE (F).

32. *The price of this merchandise fluctuates from day to day.*   32.__
     In this sentence, the word *fluctuates* means the OPPOSITE
     of *remains steady.*

33. *The patient was in acute pain.* In this sentence, the   33.__
     word *acute* means the OPPOSITE of *slight.*

34. *The essential data appear in the report.* In this   34.__
     sentence, the word *data* means the OPPOSITE of *facts.*

35. *The open lounge is spacious.* In this sentence, the word   35.__
     spacious means the OPPOSITE of *well-lighted.*

6

36. *The landscaping work was a prolonged task.* In this 36.___
    sentence, the word *prolonged* means NEARLY the same as
    difficult.

37. *A transparent removable cover was placed over the flower* 37.___
    bed. In this sentence, the word *transparent* means NEARLY
    the same as *wooden.*

38. *The prompt action of the employee saved many lives.* In 38.___
    this sentence, the word *prompt* means NEARLY the same as
    quick.

39. *The attendant's request for a vacation was approved.* In 39.___
    this sentence, the word *approved* means NEARLY the same
    as *refused.*

40. *The paycheck was received in the mail.* In this sentence, 40.___
    the word *received* means NEARLY the same as *lost.*

——

TEST 3

Questions 1-50.

DIRECTIONS: Each question consists of a statement. You are to
               indicate whether the statement is TRUE (T) or FALSE (F).
               PRINT THE LETTER OF THE CORRECT ANSWER IN THE SPACE AT
               THE RIGHT.

1. *A few men were assisting the attendant.* In this sentence, 1.___
   the word *assisting* means NEARLY the same as *helping.*

2. *He opposed the idea of using a vacuum cleaner for this job.* 2.___
   In this sentence, the word *opposed* means NEARLY the same
   as *suggested.*

3. *Four employees were selected.* In this sentence, the word 3.___
   selected means NEARLY the same as *chosen.*

4. *This man is constantly supervised.* In this sentence, the 4.___
   word *constantly* means NEARLY the same as *rarely.*

5. *One part of soap to two parts of water is sufficient.* In 5.___
   this sentence, the word *sufficient* means NEARLY the same
   as *enough.*

6. *The fire protection system was inadequate.* In this 6.___
   sentence, the word *inadequate* means NEARLY the same as
   very good.

7

7. *The nozzle of the hose was clogged.* In this sentence, the word *clogged* means NEARLY the same as *brass*.

7.__

8. *He resembles the man who worked here before.* In this sentence, the word *resembles* means NEARLY the same as *replaces*.

8.__

9. *They eliminated a number of items.* In this sentence, the word *eliminated* means NEARLY the same as *bought*.

9.__

10. *He is a dependable worker.* In this sentence, the word *dependable* means NEARLY the same as *poor*.

10.__

11. *Some wood finishes color the wood and conceal the natural grain.* In this sentence, the word *conceal* means NEARLY the same as *hide*.

11.__

12. *Paint that is chalking sometimes retains its protective value.* In this sentence, the word *retains* means NEARLY the same as *keeps*.

12.__

13. *Wood and trash had accumulated.* In this sentence, the word *accumulated* means NEARLY the same as *piled up*.

13.__

14. *An inflammable liquid is one that is easily set on fire.*

14.__

15. *The amounts were then compared.* In this sentence, the word *compared* means NEARLY the same as *added*.

15.__

16. *The boy had fallen into a shallow pool.* In this sentence, the word *shallow* means NEARLY the same as *deep*.

16.__

17. *He acquired a new instrument.* In this sentence, the word *acquired* means NEARLY the same as *got*.

17.__

18. *Several men were designated for this activity.* In this sentence, the word *designated* means NEARLY the same as *laid off*.

18.__

19. *The drawer had been converted into a file.* In this sentence, the word *converted* means NEARLY the same as *changed*.

19.__

20. *The patient has recuperated.* In this sentence, the word *recuperated* means NEARLY the same as *died*.

20.__

21. *A rigid material should be used.* In this sentence, the word *rigid* means NEARLY the same as *stiff*.

21.__

22. *Only half the supplies were utilized.* In this sentence, the word *utilized* means NEARLY the same as *used*.

22.__

23. *In all these years, he had never obstructed any change.* In this sentence, the word *obstructed* means NEARLY the same as *suggested*.

23.__

24. *Conditions were aggravated when he left.* In this sentence, the word *aggravated* means NEARLY the same as *improved*.

24.___

25. *The autopsy room is now available.* In this sentence, the word *available* means NEARLY the same as *clean*.

25.___

26. An investigation which *precedes* a report is one which comes before the report.

26.___

27. *Another word was inserted.* In this sentence, the word *inserted* means NEARLY the same as *put in*.

27.___

28. *He reversed the recommended steps in the procedure.* In this sentence, the word *reversed* means NEARLY the same as *explained*.

28.___

29. *His complaint was about a trivial matter.* In this sentence, the word *trivial* means NEARLY the same as *petty*.

29.___

30. *Using the proper tool will aid a worker in doing a better job.* In this sentence, the word *aid* means NEARLY the same as *help*.

30.___

31. *The application form has a space for the name of the former employer.* In this sentence, the word *former* means NEARLY the same as *new*.

31.___

32. *The exterior of the building needed to be painted.* In this sentence, the word *exterior* means NEARLY the same as *inside*.

32.___

33. *The smoke from the fire was dense.* In this sentence, the word *dense* means NEARLY the same as *thick*.

33.___

34. *Vacations should be planned in advance.* In this sentence, vacations should be planned ahead of time.

34.___

35. *The employee denied that he would accept another job.* In this sentence, the word *denied* means NEARLY the same as *admitted*.

35.___

36. *An annual report is made by the central stockroom.* In this sentence, the word *annual* means NEARLY the same as *monthly*.

36.___

37. *Salaries were increased in the new budget.* In this sentence, the word *increased* means NEARLY the same as *cut*.

37.___

38. *All excess oil is to be removed from tools.* In this sentence, the word *excess* means NEARLY the same as *extra*.

38.___

39. *The new employee did similar work on his last job.* In this sentence, the word *similar* means NEARLY the same as *interesting*.

39.___

9

40. *Helpful employees make favorable impressions on the public.* In this sentence, the word *favorable* means NEARLY the same as *poor*.   40.___

41. *Some plants are grown for the decorative value of their leaves.* In this sentence, the word *decorative* means NEARLY the same as *ornamental*.   41.___

42. *They made a circular flower garden.* In this sentence, the word *circular* means NEARLY the same as *square*.   42.___

43. *The gardener was a conscientious worker.* In this sentence, the word *conscientious* means NEARLY the same as *lazy*.   43.___

44. *The instructions received were contradictory.* In this sentence, the word *contradictory* means NEARLY the same as *alike*.   44.___

45. *His application for the job was rejected.* In this sentence, the word *rejected* means NEARLY the same as *accepted*.   45.___

46. *This plant reaches maturity quickly.* In this sentence, the word *maturity* means NEARLY the same as *full development*.   46.___

47. *The garden was provided with a system of underground irrigation.* In this sentence, the word *irrigation* means NEARLY the same as *watering*.   47.___

48. *In some plants, the flowers often appear before the foliage.* In this sentence, the word *foliage* refers to the leaves of the plant.   48.___

49. *The new horticultural society was organized through the merger of two previous groups.* In this sentence, the word *merger* means NEARLY the same as *breakup*.   49.___

50. *The stem of the plant measured three inches in diameter.* In this sentence, the word *diameter* means NEARLY the same as *height*.   50.___

―――

KEY (CORRECT ANSWERS)

TEST 1

1. T	11. F	21. A	31. B
2. F	12. T	22. B	32. A
3. T	13. F	23. D	33. C
4. F	14. T	24. B	34. A
5. F	15. T	25. D	35. D
6. F	16. F	26. C	36. B
7. T	17. F	27. A	37. C
8. T	18. F	28. C	38. B
9. T	19. F	29. D	39. B
10. T	20. F	30. B	40. C

TEST 2

1. B	11. B	21. D	31. A
2. A	12. C	22. A	32. T
3. C	13. B	23. D	33. T
4. B	14. D	24. C	34. F
5. A	15. C	25. D	35. F
6. D	16. B	26. B	36. F
7. B	17. D	27. D	37. F
8. B	18. D	28. B	38. T
9. A	19. A	29. A	39. F
10. C	20. A	30. C	40. F

TEST 3

1. T	11. T	21. T	31. F	41. T
2. F	12. T	22. T	32. F	42. F
3. T	13. T	23. F	33. T	43. F
4. F	14. T	24. F	34. T	44. F
5. T	15. F	25. F	35. F	45. F
6. F	16. F	26. T	36. F	46. T
7. F	17. T	27. T	37. F	47. T
8. F	18. F	28. F	38. T	48. T
9. F	19. T	29. T	39. F	49. F
10. F	20. F	30. T	40. F	50. F

BASIC WORD VOCABULARY TEST (BWVT)

COMMENTARY

Verbal ability plays a central role in intellectual development and informal human communications. It forms a basic staple of practically every test of general and mental ability.

In assessing level of development in verbal ability, a vocabulary test called the Basic Word Vocabulary Test (BWVT) has been developed.

The rationale of this test is of great importance in providing a more complete assessment of the status, health, and well-being of our population.

The test was developed to provide a measurement instrument of word-knowledge acquisition with two additional properties that are not extant in any other standardized vocabulary test. These two properties are reflected in its content representation (content validity) of a carefully specified population of words and in its range of application from about the third grade level of literacy to the highest level of word-knowledge acquisition. These two properties permit assessment of a wide range of vocabulary development in terms of absolute level (as estimates of the word population) and relative standing in reference to various normative groups, i.e., age-education standing, on one continuous scale.

Thus, this test extends measurement-capability in assessing vocabulary development practically along the full range of the psycho-social aspects of functioning.

This is the only standardized test of vocabulary that provides, in a single instrument, for the evaluation of vocabulary on the elementary, high school, college, and university levels.

EXAMINATION SECTION

DIRECTIONS: Select the word or phrase which has the same meaning, or most nearly the same meaning, as the CAPITALIZED word. *PRINT THE LETTER OF THE CORRECT ANSWER IN THE SPACE AT THE RIGHT.*

1. A CAR is to
   A. start fires with   B. eat on
   C. take pictures with   D. ride in
   E. draw with

      1.___

2. INK is used to
   A. walk on   B. write with   C. cut with
   D. serve with   E. stand on

      2.___

3. POOR means having very little
   A. money   B. hair   C. sun   D. time   E. snow

      3.___

4. COMBAT
   A. point   B. report   C. fight   D. start   E. admit

      4.___

5. A MISTAKE is something done
   A. first   B. wrong   C. next   D. often   E. alone

      5.___

6. HOWL
   A. roar   B. design   C. propose   D. depart   E. succeed

      6.___

7. PHONY
   A. tough   B. neutral   C. vivid   D. fake   E. hasty

      7.___

8. ADVICE
   A. record   B. visit   C. bridge   D. opinion   E. minute

      8.___

9. BURLAP
   A. tunnel   B. medicine   C. soil
   D. engine   E. fabric

      9.___

10. A SEAMSTRESS is a woman who
    A. writes   B. sews   C. sings   D. paints   E. bakes

      10.___

11. APPROACH means to come
    A. through   B. with   C. into   D. between   E. near

      11.___

12. ABANDON
    A. look over   B. hold on   C. lift up
    D. fall down   E. give up

      12.___

13. BARELY
    A. generally   B. scarcely   C. completely
    D. especially   E. gradually

      13.___

14. SNEER   14.___
    A. listen with interest   B. practice with care
    C. look with scorn   D. lift with ease
    E. dance with joy

15. ELIGIBLE   15.___
    A. lonesome   B. careless   C. qualified
    D. inferior   E. profound

16. EXCLUDE   16.___
    A. educate   B. excite   C. eliminate
    D. encourage   E. ensure

17. JUVENILE   17.___
    A. haunted   B. youthful   C. intimate
    D. favorable   E. unable

18. JOLT   18.___
    A. justify B. join C. judge D. jar E. journey

19. GRATIFY   19.___
    A. heat B. shout C. hope D. charge E. please

20. RAFTER   20.___
    A. angel B. canal C. beam D. lamb E. trunk

21. LANK   21.___
    A. slender   B. grateful   C. musical
    D. lively   E. rare

22. CONSOLE   22.___
    A. compare   B. conclude   C. comfort
    D. command   E. collect

23. MANIPULATE   23.___
    A. reserve   B. devote   C. handle
    D. inquire   E. introduce

24. CONCRETE   24.___
    A. clean B. mean C. low D. nice E. real

25. DESTITUTE   25.___
    A. respectful   B. divine   C. urgent
    D. slippery   E. needy

26. BASTION   26.___
    A. fortification   B. qualification   C. appropriation
    D. legislation   E. illustration

27. FOREGO   27.___
    A. represent   B. sacrifice   C. justify
    D. determine   E. display

28. MACKINTOSH   28.___
    A. raincoat   B. tractor   C. honeybee
    D. cartoon   E. saucepan

29. TRAJECTORY   29.___
    A. curved path   B. ill health
    C. bold type   D. glorious spirit
    E. strong back

30. A TRIPHTHONG is a combination of three   30.___
    A. fossils   B. cables   C. diagrams
    D. vowels   E. atoms

31. WHIST   31.___
    A. captain B. game   C. soul   D. finger   E. rock

32. FETID   32.___
    A. exhausted   B. stinking   C. pathetic
    D. meager   E. insane

33. BEZANT   33.___
    A. hotel   B. coin   C. mill   D. harbor   E. desk

34. SCINTILLATE   34.___
    A. develop B. whistle C. ruin   D. breathe E. flash

35. GLIB   35.___
    A. unaware   B. fluent   C. reluctant
    D. philosophical   E. inquisitive

36. DINT   36.___
    A. supply   B. wish   C. force   D. price   E. demand

37. SARCOPHAGUS   37.___
    A. coffin   B. insect   C. interview
    D. wharf   E. mushroom

38. DIABOLO   38.___
    A. bed   B. dance   C. game   D. mark   E. record

39. LEMPIRA   39.___
    A. chair   B. money   C. salt   D. earth   E. music

40. PYROPE   40.___
    A. reptile B. heather C. slogan D. mantle   E. garnet

KEY (CORRECT ANSWERS)

1. D	11. E	21. A	31. B
2. B	12. E	22. C	32. B
3. A	13. B	23. C	33. B
4. C	14. C	24. E	34. E
5. B	15. C	25. E	35. B
6. A	16. C	26. A	36. C
7. D	17. B	27. B	37. A
8. D	18. D	28. A	38. C
9. E	19. E	29. A	39. B
10. B	20. C	30. D	40. E

SPELLING
EXAMINATION SECTION
TEST 1

DIRECTIONS: In each of the following tests in this part, select the letter of the one MISSPELLED word in each of the following groups of words. *PRINT THE LETTER OF THE CORRECT ANSWER IN THE SPACE AT THE RIGHT.*

1. A. grateful   B. fundimental   1.___
    C. census   D. analysis

2. A. installment   B. retrieve   2.___
    C. concede   D. dissapear

3. A. accidentaly   B. dismissal   3.___
    C. conscientious   D. indelible

4. A. perceive   B. carreer   C. anticipate   D. acquire   4.___

5. A. facillity   B. reimburse   C. assortment   D. guidance   5.___

6. A. plentiful   B. across   6.___
    C. advantagous   D. similar

7. A. omission   B. pamphlet   C. guarrantee   D. repel   7.___

8. A. maintenance   B. always   8.___
    C. liable   D. anouncement

9. A. exaggerate   B. sieze   C. condemn   D. commit   9.___

10. A. pospone   B. altogether   C. grievance   D. excessive   10.___

11. A. banana   B. trafic   C. spectacle   D. boundary   11.___

12. A. commentator   B. abbreviation   12.___
    C. battaries   D. monastery

13. A. practically   B. advise   13.___
    C. pursuade   D. laboratory

14. A. fatigueing   B. invincible   14.___
    C. strenuous   D. ceiling

15. A. propeller   B. reverence   C. piecemeal   D. underneth   15.___

16. A. annonymous   B. envelope   C. transit   D. variable   16.___

17. A. petroleum   B. bigoted   C. meager   D. resistence   17.___

18. A. permissible   B. indictment   18.___
    C. fundemental   D. nowadays

19.   A. thief   B. bargin   C. nuisance   D. vacant   19.__

20.   A. technique   B. vengeance   C. aquatic   D. heighth   20.__

TEST 2

1.   A. apparent   B. superintendent   1.__
     C. releive   D. calendar

2.   A. foreign   B. negotiate C. typical   D. disipline   2.__

3.   A. posponed   B. argument   3.__
     C. susceptible   D. deficit

4.   A. preferred   B. column   C. peculiar   D. equiped   4.__

5.   A. exaggerate   B. disatisfied   5.__
     C. repetition   D. already

6.   A. livelihood   B. physician C. obsticle   D. strategy   6.__

7.   A. courageous   B. ommission C. ridiculous   D. awkward   7.__

8.   A. sincerely   B. abundance C. negligable   D. elementary 8.__

9.   A. obsolete   B. mischievous   9.__
     C. enumerate   D. atheletic

10. A. fiscel   B. beneficiary   10.__
     C. concede   D. translate

11. A. segregate   B. excessivly C. territory   D. obstacle   11.__

12. A. unnecessary   B. monopolys   12.__
     C. harmonious   D. privilege

13. A. sinthetic   B. intellectual   13.__
     C. gracious   D. archaic

14. A. beneficial   B. fulfill   C. sarcastic   D. disolve   14.__

15. A. umbrella   B. sentimental   15.__
     C. inefficent   D. psychiatrist

16. A. noticable   B. knapsack   C. librarian   D. meant   16.__

17. A. conference   B. upheaval   C. vulger   D. odor

18. A. surmount   B. pentagon   C. calorie   D. inumerable 18.__

19. A. classifiable   B. moisturize   19.__
     C. monitor   D. assesment

20. A. thermastat   B. corrupting C. approach   D. thinness   20

2

TEST 3

1. A. typical   B. descend   C. summarize   D. continuel   1.___
2. A. courageous   B. recomend   C. omission   D. eliminate   2.___
3. A. compliment   B. illuminate   3.___
    C. auxilary   D. installation
4. A. preliminary   B. aquainted   4.___
    C. syllable   D. analysis
5. A. accustomed   B. negligible   C. interupted   D. bulletin   5.___
6. A. summoned   B. managment   C. mechanism   D. sequence   6.___
7. A. commitee   B. surprise   C. noticeable   D. emphasize   7.___
8. A. occurrance   B. likely   C. accumulate   D. grievance   8.___
9. A. obstacle   B. particuliar   9.___
    C. baggage   D. fascinating
10. A. innumerable   B. seize   10.___
    C. applicant   D. dictionery
11. A. monkeys   B. rigid   C. unnatural   D. roomate   11.___
12. A. surveying   B. figurative   C. famous   D. curiosety   12.___
13. A. rodeo   B. inconcievable   13.___
    C. calendar   D. magnificence
14. A. handicaped   B. glacier   C. defiance   D. emperor   14.___
15. A. schedule   B. scrawl   C. seclusion   D. sissors   15.___
16. A. tissues   B. tomatos   C. tyrants   D. tragedies   16.___
17. A. casette   B. graceful   C. penicillin   D. probably   17.___
18. A. gnawed   B. microphone   C. clinicle   D. batch   18.___
19. A. amateur   B. altitude   C. laborer   D. expence   19.___
20. A. mandate   B. flexable   C. despise   D. verify   20.___

TEST 4

1. A. primery   B. mechanic   C. referred   D. admissible   1.___
2. A. cessation   B. beleif   C. aggressive   D. allowance   2.___
3. A. leisure   B. authentic   3.___
    C. familiar   D. contemptable

3

4. A. volume   B. forty   C. dilemma   D. seldum   4.__

5. A. discrepancy   B. aquisition   5.__
    C. exorbitant   D. lenient

6. A. simultanous   B. penetrate   6.__
    C. revision   D. conspicuous

7. A. ilegible   B. gracious   C. profitable   D. obedience   7.__

8. A. manufacturer   B. authorize   8.__
    C. compelling   D. pecular

9. A. anxious   B. rehearsal   C. handicaped   D. tendency   9.__

10. A. meticulous   B. accompaning   10.__
    C. initiative   D. shelves

11. A. hammaring   B. insecticide   11.__
    C. capacity   D. illogical

12. A. budget   B. luminous   C. aviation   D. lunchon   12.__

13. A. moniter   B. bachelor   13.__
    C. pleasurable   D. omitted

14. A. monstrous   B. transistor   C. narrative   D. anziety   14.__

15. A. engagement   B. judical   C. pasteurize   D. tried   15.__

16. A. fundimental   B. innovation   16.__
    C. perpendicular   D. extravagant

17. A. bookkeeper   B. brutality   C. gymnaseum   D. cemetery   17.__

18. A. sturdily   B. pretentious   18.__
    C. gourmet   D. enterance

19. A. resturant   B. tyranny   19.__
    C. kindergarten   D. ancestry

20. A. benefit   B. possess   C. speciman   D. noticing   20.__

_____

TEST 5

1. A. arguing   B. correspondance   1.__
    C. forfeit   D. dissension

2. A. occasion   B. description   2.__
    C. prejudice   D. elegible

3. A. accomodate   B. initiative   C. changeable   D. enroll   3.__

4.   A. temporary   B. insistent   C. benificial   D. separate   4.___

5.   A. achieve   B. dissappoint   5.___
     C. unanimous   D. judgment

6.   A. procede   B. publicly   C. sincerity   D. successful   6.___

7.   A. deceive   B. goverment   C. preferable   D. repetitive   7.___

8.   A. emphasis   B. skillful   C. advisible   D. optimistic   8.___

9.   A. tendency   B. rescind   C. crucial   D. noticable   9.___

10. A. privelege   B. abbreviate   C. simplify   D. divisible   10.___

11. A. irresistible   B. varius   11.___
     C. mutual   D. refrigerator

12. A. amateur   B. distinguish   12.___
     C. rehearsal   D. poision

13. A. biased   B. ommission   C. precious   D. coordinate 13.___

14. A. calculated   B.enthusiasm   C. sincerely   D. parashute 14.___

15. A. sentry   B. materials   C. incredable   D. budget   15.___

16. A. chocolate   B. instrument   C. volcanoe   D. shoulder   16.___

17. A. ancestry   B. obscure   C. intention   D. ninty   17.___

18. A. artical   B. bracelet   C. beggar   D. hopeful   18.___

19. A. tournament   B. sponsor   19.___
     C. perpendiclar   D. dissolve

20. A. yeild   B. physician   C. greasiest   D. admitting   20.___

TEST 6

1.   A. achievment   B. maintenance   1.___
     C. questionnaire   D. all are correct

2.   A. prevelant   B. pronunciation   2.___
     C. separate   D. all are correct

3.   A. permissible   B. relevant   3.___
     C. seize   D. all are correct

4.   A. corroborate   B. desparate   4.___
     C. eighth   D. all are correct

5. A. exceed   B. feasibility   5.___
    C. psycological   D. all are correct

6. A. parallel   B. aluminum   C. calendar   D. eigty   6.___

7. A. microbe   B. ancient   C. autograph   D. existance   7.___

8. A. plentiful   B. skillful   C. amoung   D. capsule   8.___

9. A. erupt   B. quanity   C. opinion   D. competent   9.___

10. A. excitement B. discipline C. luncheon   D. regreting   10.___

11. A. magazine   B. expository C. imitation   D. permenent   11.___

12. A. ferosious   B. machinery   12.___
    C. precise   D. magnificent

13. A. conceive   B. narritive   C. separation D. management   13.___

14. A. muscular   B. witholding C. pickle   D. glacier   14.___

15. A. vehicel   B. mismanage   15.___
    C. correspondence   D. dissatisfy

16. A. sentince   B. bulletin   C. notice   D. definition   16.___

17. A. appointment   B. exactly   17.___
    C. typest   D. light

18. A. penalty   B. suparvise   C. consider   D. division   18.___

19. A. schedule   B. accurate   C. corect   D. simple   19.___

20. A. suggestion B. installed   C. proper   D. agincy   20.___

TEST 7

1. A. symtom   B. serum   C. antiseptic D. aromatic   1.___

2. A. register   B. registrar   C. purser   D. burser   2.___

3. A. athletic   B. tragedy   C. batallion   D. sophomore   3.___

4. A. latent   B. godess   C. aisle   D. whose   4.___

5. A. rhyme   B. rhythm   C. thime   D. thine   5.___

6. A. eighth   B. exaggerate C. electorial D. villain   6.___

7. A. statute   B. superintendent   · 7.___
    C. iresistible   D. colleague

6

8. A. sieze   B. therefor   C. auxiliary   D. changeable   8. ___

9. A. siege   B. knowledge   C. lieutenent   D. weird   9. ___

10. A. acquitted   B. polititian   C. professor   D. conqueror   10. ___

11. A. changeable   B. chargeable   C. salable   D. useable   11. ___

12. A. promissory   B. prisoner   C. excellent   D. tyrrany   12. ___

13. A. conspicuous   B. essance   13. ___
    C. comparative   D. brilliant

14. A. notefying   B. accentuate   C. adhesive   D. primarily   14. ___

15. A. exercise   B. sublime   C. stuborn   D. shameful   15. ___

16. A. presume   B. transcript   C. strech   D. wizard   16. ___

17. A. specify   B. regional   17. ___
    C. arbitrary   D. segragation

18. A. requirement   B. happiness   18. ___
    C. achievement   D. gentlely

19. A. endurance   B. fusion   C. balloon   D. enormus   19. ___

20. A. luckily   B. schedule   C. simplicity   D. sanwich   20. ___

TEST 8

1. A. maintain   B. maintainance   1. ___
   C. sustain   D. sustenance

2. A. portend   B. portentious   2. ___
   C. pretend   D. pretentious

3. A. prophesize   B. prophesies   3. ___
   C. farinaceous   D. spaceous

4. A. choose   B. chose   C. choosen   D. chasten   4. ___

5. A. censure   B. censorious   5. ___
   C. pleasure   D. pleasurible

6. A. cover   B. coverage   C. adder   D. adege   6. ___

7. A. balloon   B. diregible   C. direct   D. descent   7. ___

8. A. whemsy   B. crazy   C. flimsy   D. lazy   8. ___

9. A. derision   B. pretention   C. sustention   D. contention   9. ___

| 10. | A. question | | B. questionaire | | 10.__ |
| | C. legion | | D. legionary | | |

| 11. | A. chattle | B. cattle | C. dismantle | D. kindle | 11.__ |

| 12. | A. canal | B. cannel | C. chanel | D. colonel | 12.__ |

| 13. | A. hemorrage | B. storage | C. manage | D. foliage | 13.__ |

| 14. | A. surgeon | B. sturgeon | C. luncheon | D. stancheon | 14.__ |

| 15. | A. diploma | B. commission | C. dependent | D. luminious | 15.__ |

| 16. | A. likelihood | B. blizzard | C. machanical | D. suppress | 16.__ |

| 17. | A. commercial | B. releif | C. disposal | D. endeavor | 17.__ |

| 18. | A. operate | B. bronco | C. excaping | D. grammar | 18.__ |

| 19. | A. orchard | B. collar | C. embarass | D. distant | 19.__ |

| 20. | A. sincerly | B. possessive | C. weighed | D. waist | 20.__ |

TEST 9

| 1. | A. statute | | B. stationary | | 1.__ |
| | C. staturesque | | D. stature | | |

| 2. | A. practicible | | B. practical | | 2.__ |
| | C. particle | | D. reticule | | |

| 3. | A. plague | B. plaque | C. ague | D. aigrete | 3.__ |

| 4. | A. theology | B. idealogy | C. psychology | D. philology | 4.__ |

| 5. | A. dilema | B. stamina | C. feminine | D. strychnine | 5.__ |

| 6. | A. deceit | B. benefit | C. grieve | D. hienous | 6.__ |

| 7. | A. commensurable | | B. measurable | | 7.__ |
| | C. duteable | | D. salable | | |

| 8. | A. homogeneous | | B. heterogeneous | | 8.__ |
| | C. advantageous | | D. religeous | | |

| 9. | A. criticize | B. dramatise | C. exorcise | D. exercise | 9.__ |

| 10. | A. ridiculous | B. comparable | C. merciful | D. cotten | 10.__ |

| 11. | A. antebiotic | B. stitches | C. pitiful | D. sneaky | 11.__ |

| 12. | A. amendment | | B. candadate | | 12.__ |
| | C. accountable | | D. recommendation | | |

13.   A. avocado   B. recruit   C. tripping   D. probally   13.___

14.   A. calendar   B. desirable   C. familar   D. vacuum   14.___

15.   A. deteriorate   B. elligible   15.___
      C. liable   D. missile

16.   A. amateur   B. competent   16.___
      C. mischeivous   D. occasion

17.   A. friendliness   B. saleries   17.___
      C. cruelty   D. ammunition

18.   A. wholesome   B. cieling   C. stupidity   D. eligible   18.___

19.   A. comptroller   B. traveled   19.___
      C. accede   D. procede

20.   A. Britain   B. Brittainica   20.___
      C. conductor   D. vendor

TEST 10

1.   A. lengthen   B. region   C. gases   D. inspecter   1.___

2.   A. imediately   B. forbidden   2.___
      C. complimentary   D. aeronautics

3.   A. continuous   B. paralel   C. opposite   D. definite   3.___

4.   A. Antarctic   B. Wednesday   C. Febuary   D. Hungary   4.___

5.   A. transmission   B. exposure   5.___
      C. pistol   D. customery

6.   A. juvinile   B. martyr   6.___
      C. deceive   D. collaborate

7.   A. unnecessary   B. repetitive   7.___
      C. cancellation   D. airey

8.   A. transit   B. availible   C. objection   D. galaxy   8.___

9.   A. ineffective   B. believeable   9.___
      C. arrangement   D. aggravate

10.   A. possession   B. progress   C. reception   D. predjudice   10.___

11.   A. congradulate   B. percolate   11.___
      C. major   D. leisure

12.   A. convenience   B. privilige   12.___
      C. emerge   D. immerse

13. A. erasable   B. inflammable   13.__
    C. audable   D. laudable

14. A. final   B. fines   C. finis   D. Finish   14.__

15. A. emitted   B. representative   15.__
    C. discipline   D. insistance

16. A. diphthong   B. rarified   C. library   D. recommend   16.__

17. A. compel   B. belligerent   17.__
    C. successful   D. sargeant

18. A. dispatch   B. dispise   C. dispose   D. dispute   18.__

19. A. administrator   B. adviser   19.__
    C. diner   D. celluler

20. A. ignite   B. ignision   C. igneous   D. ignited   20.__

TEST 11

1. A. repellent   B. secession   C. sebaceous   D. saxaphone   1.__

2. A. navel   B. counteresolution   2.__
    C. marginalia   D. perceptible

3. A. Hammerskjold   B. Nehru   3.__
    C. U Thamt   D. Khrushchev

4. A. perculate   B. periwinkle   4.__
    C. perigee   D. retrogression

5. A. buccaneer   B. tobacco   C. Buffalo   D. oscilate   5.__

6. A. siege   B. wierd   C. seize   D. cemetery   6.__

7. A. equaled   B. bigoted   7.__
    C. benefited   D. kaleideoscope

8. A. blamable   B. bullrush   8.__
    C. questionnaire   D. irascible

9. A. tobagganed   B. acquiline   9.__
    C. capillary   D. cretonne

10. A. daguerrotype   B. elegiacal   10.__
    C. iridescent   D. inchoate

11. A. bayonet   B. braggadocio   11.__
    C. corollary   D. connoiseur

12.   A. equinoctial   B. fusillade   12.___
      C. fricassee   D. potpouri

13.   A. octameter   B. impressario   13.___
      C. hyetology   D. hieroglyphics

14.   A. innanity   B. idyllic   C. fylfot   D. inimical   14.___

15.   A. liquefy   B. rarefy   C. putrify   D. sapphire   15.___

16.   A. canonical   B. stupified   16.___
      C. millennium   D. memorabilia

17.   A. paraphenalia   B. odyssey   17.___
      C. onomatopoeia   D. osseous

18.   A. peregrinate   B. pecadillo   18.___
      C. reptilian   D. uxorious

19.   A. pharisaical   B. vicissitude   19.___
      C. puissance   D. wainright

20.   A. holocaust   B. tesselate   C. scintilla   D. staccato   20.___

TEST 12

1.   A. questionnaire   B. gondoleer   1.___
     C. chandelier   D. acquiescence

2.   A. surveillence   B. surfeit   2.___
     C. vaccinate   D. belligerent

3.   A. occassionally   B. recurrence   3.___
     C. silhouette   D. incessant

4.   A. transferral   B. benefical   4.___
     C. descendent   D. dependent

5.   A. separately   B. flouresence   5.___
     C. deterrent   D. parallel

6.   A. acquittal   B. enforceable   6.___
     C. counterfeit   D. indispensible

7.   A. susceptible   B. accelarate   7.___
     C. exhilarate   D. accommodation

8.   A. impedimenta   B. collateral   8.___
     C. liason   D. epistolary

9.   A. inveigle   B. panegyric   C. reservoir   D. manuver   9.___

10. A. synopsis   B. parephernalia   10._
     C. affidavit   D. subpoena

11. A. grosgrain   B. vermilion   C. abbatoir   D. connoiseur   11._

12. A. gabardine   B. camoflage   C. hemorrhage   D. contraband   12._

13. A. opprobrious   B. defalcate   13._
     C. fiduciery   D. recommendations

14. A. nebulous   B. necessitate   14._
     C. impricate   D. discrepancy

15. A. discrete   B. condesension   15._
     C. condign   D. condiment

16. A. cavalier   B. effigy   16._
     C. legitimatly   D. misalliance

17. A. rheumatism   B. vaporous   17._
     C. cannister   D. hallucinations

18. A. paleonthology   B. octogenarian   18._
     C. gradient   D. impingement

19. A. fusilade   B. fusilage   C. ensilage   D. desiccate   19._

20. A. rationale   B. raspberry   C. reprobate   D. varigated   20._

─────────

KEY (CORRECT ANSWERS)

TEST 1

1. B. fundamental
2. D. disappear
3. A. accidentally
4. B. career
5. A. facility

6. C. advantageous
7. C. guarantee
8. D. announcement
9. B. seize
10. A. postpone

11. B. traffic
12. C. batteries
13. C. persuade
14. A. fatiguing
15. D. underneath

16. A. anonymous
17. D. resistance
18. C. fundamental
19. B. bargain
20. D. height

TEST 2

1. C. relieve
2. D. discipline
3. A. postponed
4. D. equipped
5. B. dissatisfied

6. C. obstacle
7. B. omission
8. C. negligible
9. D. athletic
10. A. fiscal

11. B. excessively
12. B. monopolies
13. A. synthetic
14. D. dissolve
15. C. inefficient

16. A. noticeable
17. C. vulgar
18. D. innumerable
19. D. assessment
20. A. thermostat

TEST 3

1. D. continual
2. B. recommend
3. C. auxiliary
4. B. acquainted
5. C. interrupted

6. B. management
7. A. committee
8. A. occurrence
9. B. particular
10. D. dictionary

11. D. roommate
12. D. curiosity
13. B. inconceivable
14. A. handicapped
15. D. scissors

16. B. tomatoes
17. A. cassette
18. C. clinical
19. D. expense
20. B. flexible

TEST 4

1. A. primary
2. B. belief
3. D. contemptible
4. D. seldom
5. B. acquisition

6. A. simultaneous
7. A. illegible
8. D. peculiar
9. C. handicapped
10. B. accompanying

11. A. hammering
12. D. luncheon
13. A. monitor
14. D. anxiety
15. B. judicial

16. A. fundamental
17. C. gymnasium
18. D. entrance
19. A. restaurant
20. C. specimen

TEST 5

1. B. correspondence
2. D. eligible
3. A. accommodate
4. C. beneficial
5. B. disappoint

6. A. proceed
7. B. government
8. C. advisable
9. D. noticeable
10. A. privilege

11. B. various
12. D. poison
13. B. omission
14. D. parachute
15. C. incredible

16. C. volcano
17. D. ninety
18. A. article
19. C. perpendicular
20. A. yield

TEST 6

1. A. achievement
2. A. prevalent
3. D all are correct
4. B. desperate
5. C. psychological

6. D. eighty
7. D. existence
8. C. among
9. B. quantity
10. D. regretting

11. D. permanent
12. A. ferocious
13. B. narrative
14. B. withholding
15. A. vehicle

16. A. sentence
17. C. typist
18. B. supervise
19. C. correct
20. D. agency

TEST 7

1. A. symptom
2. D. bursar
3. C. battalion
4. B. goddess
5. C. thyme

6. C. electoral
7. C. irresistible
8. A. seize
9. C. lieutenant
10. B. politician

11. D. usable
12. D. tyrany
13. B. essence
14. A. notifying
15. C. stubborn

16. C. stretch
17. D. segregation
18. D. gently
19. D. enormous
20. D. sandwich

TEST 8

1. B. maintenance
2. B. portentous
3. D. spacious
4. C. chosen
5. D. pleasurable

6. D. adage
7. B. dirigible
8. A. whimsy
9. B. pretension
10. B. questionnaire

11. A. chattel
12. C. channel
13. A. hemorrhage
14. D. stanchion
15. D. luminous

16. C. mechanical
17. B. relief
18. C. escaping
19. C. embarrass
20. A. sincerely

TEST 9

1. C. statuesque
2. A. practicable
3. D. aigrette
4. B. ideology
5. A. dilemma

6. D. heinous
7. C. dutiable
8. D. religious
9. B. dramatize
10. D. cotton

11. A. antibiotic
12. B. candidate
13. D. probably
14. C. familiar
15. B. eligible

16. C. mischievous
17. B. salaries
18. B. ceiling
19. D. proceed
20. B. Brittanica

TEST 10

1. D. inspector
2. A. immediately
3. B. parallel
4. C. February
5. D. customary

6. A. juvenile
7. D. airy
8. B. available
9. B. believable
10. D. prejudice

11. A. congratulate
12. B. privilege
13. C. audible
14. D. Finnish
15. D. insistence

16. B. rarefied
17. D. sergeant
18. B. despise
19. D. cellular
20. B. ignition

TEST 11

1. D. saxophone
2. B. counterresolution
3. C. U Thant
4. A. percolate
5. D. oscillate

6. B. weird
7. D. kaleidoscope
8. B. bulrush
9. B. aquiline
10. A. daguerreotype

11. D. connoisseur
12. D. potpourri
13. B. impresario
14. A. inanity
15. C. putrefy

16. B. stupefied
17. A. paraphernalia
18. B. peccadillo
19. D. wainwright
20. B. tessellate

TEST 12

1. B. gondolier
2. A. surveillance
3. A. occasionally
4. B. beneficial
5. B. fluorescence

6. D. indispensable
7. B. accelerate
8. C. liaison
9. D. maneuver
10. B. paraphernalia

11. D. connoisseur
12. B. camouflage
13. C. fiduciary
14. C. imprecate
15. B. condescension

16. C. legitimately
17. C. canister
18. A. paleontology
19. A. fusillade
20. D. variegated

VERBAL ANALOGIES

EXAMINATION SECTION

TEST 1

DIRECTIONS: In Questions 1 to 10, the first two *italicized* words have a relationship to each other. Determine that relationship, and then match the third *italicized* word with the one of the lettered choices with which it has the same relationship as the words of the first pair have to each other. *PRINT THE LETTER OF THE CORRECT ANSWER IN THE SPACE AT THE RIGHT.*

In order to help you understand the procedure, a sample question is given:

SAMPLE: *dog* is to *bark* as *cat* is to
      A. animal   B. small   C. meow
      D. pet   E. snarl

The relationship between *dog* and *bark* is that the sound which a dog normally emits is a bark. In the same way, the sound which a cat emits is a meow. Thus, C is the CORRECT answer.

1. *Fine* is to *speeding* as *jail* is to   1.___
   A. bars   B. prisoner   C. warden
   D. confinement   E. steal

2. *Orchid* is to *rose* as *gold* is to   2.___
   A. watch   B. copper   C. mine   D. coin   E. mint

3. *Pistol* is to *machine gun* as *button* is to   3.___
   A. coat   B. bullet   C. zipper
   D. tailor   E. needle and thread

4. *Spontaneous* is to *unrehearsed* as *planned* is to 4.___
   A. completed   B. organized   C. restricted
   D. understood   E. informal

5. *Friendly* is to *hostile* as *loyalty* is to   5.___
   A. fealty   B. evil   C. devotion
   D. warlike   E. treachery

6. *Fear* is to *flight* as *bravery* is to   6.___
   A. courage   B. danger   C. resistance
   D. injury   E. unyielding

7. *Economical* is to *stingy* as *sufficient* is to   7.___
   A. abundant   B. adequate   C. expensive
   D. needy   E. greedy

8. *Astronomer* is to *observation* as *senator* is to 8.___
   A. caucus   B. election   C. convention
   D. legislation   E. patronage

9. *Hunger* is to *food* as *exhaustion* is to   9.___
    A. labor   B. play   C. illness
    D. debility   E. rest

10. *Entertainment* is to *boredom* as *efficiency* is to   10.___
    A. ignorance   B. government   C. waste
    D. expert   E. time and motion studies

———

KEY (CORRECT ANSWERS)

1. E	6. C
2. B	7. A
3. C	8. D
4. B	9. E
5. E	10. C

———

TEST 2

DIRECTIONS: In Questions 1 to 10, the first two *italicized* words have a relationship to each other. Determine that relationship, and then match the third *italicized* word with the one of the lettered choices with which it has the same relationship as the words of the first pair have to each other. *PRINT THE LETTER OF THE CORRECT ANSWER IN THE SPACE AT THE RIGHT.*

1. *Diamond* is to *glass* as *platinum* is to   1.___
   A. jewelry   B. metal   C. aluminum
   D. mine   E. white

2. *Water* is to *aqueduct* as *electricity* is to   2.___
   A. meter   B. battery   C. fuse   D. wire   E. solenoid

3. *Oratory* is to *filibuster* as *reign* is to   3.___
   A. tyrant   B. terror   C. government
   D. bluster   E. confusion

4. *Gravity* is to *gaiety* as *taunt* is to   4.___
   A. ridicule   B. console   C. avoid
   D. amuse   E. condone

5. *Electron* is to *atom* as *earth* is to   5.___
   A. sun   B. solar system   C. moon
   D. planet   E. center

6. *Flattery* is to *adulation* as *cruelty* is to   6.___
   A. pain   B. barbarity   C. censorious
   D. compassion   E. duality

7. *Rowboat* is to *oar* as *automobile* is to   7.___
   A. land   B. engine   C. driver
   D. passenger   E. piston

8. *Friction* is to *oil* as *war* is to   8.___
   A. conference   B. peace   C. munitions
   D. satellite   E. retaliation

9. *Disease* is to *infection* as *reaction* is to   9.___
   A. control   B. injury   C. relapse
   D. stipulation   E. sensation

10. *Persecution* is to *martyr* as *swindle* is to   10.___
    A. embezzler   B. refuge   C. confidence man
    D. bank   E. dupe

KEY (CORRECT ANSWERS)

1. C		6. B	
2. D		7. B	
3. E		8. A	
4. B		9. E	
5. B		10. E	

TEST 3

DIRECTIONS: In Questions 1 to 10, the first two *italicized* words have a relationship to each other. Determine that relationship, and then match the third *italicized* word with the one of the lettered choices with which it has the same relationship as the words of the first pair have to each other. *PRINT THE LETTER OF THE CORRECT ANSWER IN THE SPACE AT THE RIGHT.*

1. *Woman* is to *man* as *Mary* is to   1.____
   A. woman   B. child   C. female   D. John   E. male

2. *Land* is to *ocean* as *soldier* is to   2.____
   A. river   B. sailor   C. shore   D. uniform   E. sailing

3. *Sugar* is to *candy* as *flour* is to   3.____
   A. eat   B. cook   C. candy   D. bread   E. sweet

4. *Sorrow* is to *joy* as *laugh* is to   4.____
   A. amuse   B. tears   C. fun   D. weep   E. cry

5. *Heat* is to *fire* as *pain* is to   5.____
   A. injury   B. wind   C. weather   D. cool   E. summer

6. *Grass* is to *cattle* as *milk* is to   6.____
   A. growing   B. lawn   C. baby   D. green   E. sun

7. *Winter* is to *spring* as *autumn* is to   7.____
   A. summer   B. winter   C. warm   D. cold   E. flower

8. *Rising* is to *falling* as *smile* is to   8.____
   A. climbing   B. baking   C. scolding
   D. frown   E. laughing

9. *Day* is to *night* as *succeed* is to   9.____
   A. fail   B. sunshine   C. evening
   D. afternoon   E. morning

10. *Apple* is to *fruit* as *corn* is to   10.____
    A. orange   B. eat   C. grain   D. cereal   E. food

KEY (CORRECT ANSWERS)

1. D		6. C	
2. B		7. B	
3. D		8. D	
4. E		9. A	
5. A		10. C	

TEST 4

DIRECTIONS: In Questions 1 to 10, the first two *italicized* words have a relationship to each other. Determine that relationship, and then match the third *italicized* word with the one of the lettered choices with which it has the same relationship as the words of the first pair have to each other. *PRINT THE LETTER OF THE CORRECT ANSWER IN THE SPACE AT THE RIGHT.*

1. *Robin* is to *feathers* as *cat* is to   1.___
    A. sing   B. fur   C. eat   D. bird   E. fly

2. *Late* is to *end* as *early* is to   2.___
    A. prompt   B. enter   C. begin   D. start   E. end

3. *Beginning* is to *end* as *horse* is to   3.___
    A. cart   B. automobile   C. wagon
    D. travel   E. ride

4. *Kitten* is to *cat* as *baby* is to   4.___
    A. rabbit   B. mother   C. dog   D. cow   E. lamb

5. *Little* is to *weak* as *big* is to   5.___
    A. boy   B. man   C. tall   D. baby   E. strong

6. *Arm* is to *hand* as *leg* is to   6.___
    A. knee   B. toe   C. elbow   D. foot   E. finger

7. *Alive* is to *dead* as *well* is to   7.___
    A. grow   B. sick   C. decay   D. sleep   E. play

8. *In* is to *out* as *bad* is to   8.___
    A. up   B. open   C. good   D. shut   E. on

9. *Dust* is to *dry* as *mud* is to   9.___
    A. wet   B. blow   C. splash   D. fly   E. settle

10. *Width* is to *wide* as *height* is to   10.___
    A. high   B. low   C. tall   D. brief   E. short

KEY (CORRECT ANSWERS)

1. B		6. D	
2. C		7. B	
3. A		8. C	
4. B		9. A	
5. E		10. C	

TEST 5

DIRECTIONS: In Questions 1 to 10, the first two *italicized* words have a relationship to each other. Determine that relationship, and then match the third *italicized* word with the one of the lettered choices with which it has the same relationship as the words of the first pair have to each other. *PRINT THE LETTER OF THE CORRECT ANSWER IN THE SPACE AT THE RIGHT.*

1. *Above* is to *below* as *before* is to   1.____
   A. beyond   B. behind   C. beside   D. between   E. after

2. *Start* is to *stop* as *begin* is to   2.____
   A. go   B. run   C. wait   D. finish   E. work

3. *Everything* is to *nothing* as *always* is to   3.____
   A. forever   B. usually   C. never
   D. sometimes   E. something

4. *Search* is to *find* as *question* is to   4.____
   A. answer   B. reply   C. study
   D. problem   E. explain

5. *Top* is to *spin* as *spear* is to   5.____
   A. bottom   B. roll   C. throw   D. sharp   E. pin

6. *Scale* is to *weight* as *thermometer* is to   6.____
   A. weather   B. temperature   C. pounds
   D. spring   E. chronometer

7. *Congress* is to *senator* as *convention* is to   7.____
   A. election   B. chairman   C. delegate
   D. nominee   E. representative

8. *Dividend* is to *investor* as *wage* is to   8.____
   A. employee   B. salary   C. consumer
   D. price   E. employer

9. *Terminate* is to *commence* as *adjourn* is to   9.____
   A. enact   B. convene   C. conclude
   D. veto   E. prorogue

10. *Administrator* is to *policy* as *clerk* is to   10.____
    A. subornation   B. organization   C. coordination
    D. direction   E. application

KEY (CORRECT ANSWERS)

1. E	6. B
2. D	7. C
3. C	8. A
4. A	9. B
5. C	10. E

READING COMPREHENSION
UNDERSTANDING AND INTERPRETING WRITTEN MATERIAL
COMMENTARY

The ability to read and understand written materials -- texts, publications, newspapers, orders, directions, expositions -- is a skill basic to a functioning democracy and to an efficient business or viable government.

That is why almost all examinations -- for beginning, middle, and senior levels -- test reading comprehension, directly or indirectly.

The reading test measures how well you understand what you read. This is how it is done: You read a short paragraph and five statements. From the five statements, you choose the one statement, or answer, that is BEST supported by, or best matches, what is said in the paragraph.

SAMPLE QUESTIONS

DIRECTIONS: Each question has five suggested answers, lettered A,B,C,D, and E. Decide which one is the BEST answer. *PRINT THE LETTER OF THE CORRECT ANSWER IN THE SPACE AT THE RIGHT.*

1. The prevention of accidents makes it necessary not only that safety devices be used to guard exposed machinery but also that mechanics be instructed in safety rules which they must follow for their own protection and that the light in the plant be adequate.
   The paragraph BEST supports the statement that industrial accidents
   A. are always avoidable
   B. may be due to ignorance
   C. usually result from inadequate machinery
   D. cannot be entirely overcome
   E. result in damage to machinery

ANALYSIS

Remember what you have to do --
   First - Read the paragraph.
   Second - Decide what the paragraph means.
   Third - Read the five suggested answers.
   Fourth - Select the one answer which BEST matches what the paragraph says or is BEST supported by something in the paragraph. (Sometimes you may have to read the paragraph again in order to be sure which suggested answer is best.)

This paragraph is talking about three steps that should be taken to prevent industrial accidents --
   1. use safety devices on machines
   2. instruct mechanics in safety rules
   3. provide adequate lighting.

SELECTION

With this in mind let's look at each suggested answer. Each one starts with "Industrial accidents ..."

SUGGESTED ANSWER A.
   Industrial accidents (A) are always avoidable.
   (The paragraph talks about how to avoid accidents, but does not say that accidents are always avoidable.)

1

SUGGESTED ANSWER B.

Industrial accidents (b) may be due to ignorance.

(One of the steps given in the paragraph to prevent accidents is to instruct mechanics on safety rules. This suggests that lack of knowledge or ignorance of safety rules causes accidents. This suggested answer sounds like a good possibility for being the right answer.)

SUGGESTED ANSWER C.

Industrial accidents (C) usually result from inadequate machinery.

(The paragraph does suggest that exposed machines cause accidents, but it doesn't say that it is the usual cause of accidents. The word *usually* makes this a wrong answer.)

SUGGESTED ANSWER D.

Industrial accidents (D) cannot be entirely overcome.

(You may know from your own experience that this is a true statement. But that is not what the paragraph is talking about. Therefore it is NOT the correct answer.)

SUGGESTED ANSWER E.

Industrial accidents (E) result in damage to machinery.

(This is a statement that may or may not be true, but in any case it is NOT covered by the paragraph.)

Looking back, you see that the one suggested answer of the five given that BEST matches what the paragraph says is --

Industrial accidents (B) may be due to ignorance.

The CORRECT answer then is B.

Be sure you read ALL the possible answers before you make your choice. You may think that none of the five answers is really good, but choose the BEST one of the five.

2. Probably few people realize, as they drive on a concrete road, that steel is used to keep the surface flat in spite of the weight of the busses and trucks. Steel bars, deeply embedded in the concrete, provide sinews to take the stresses so that the stresses cannot crack the slab or make it wavy.

The paragraph BEST supports the statement THAT a concrete road
   A. is expensive to build
   B. usually cracks under heavy weights
   C. looks like any other road
   D. is used only for heavy traffic
   E. is reinforced with other material

ANALYSIS

This paragraph is commenting on the fact that --
   1. few people realize, as they drive on a concrete road, that steel is deeply embedded
   2. steel keeps the surface flat
   3. steel bars enable the road to take the stresses without cracking or becoming wavy.

SELECTION

Now read and think about the possible answers:
   A. A concrete road is expensive to build.
      (Maybe so but that is not what the paragraph is about.)
   B. A concrete road usually cracks under heavy weights.
      (The paragraph talks about using steel bars to prevent heavy weights from cracking concrete roads. It says nothing about how usual it is for the roads to crack. The word *usually* makes this suggested answer wrong.)

2

C. A concrete road looks like any other road.
   (This may or may not be true. The important thing to note is that
   it has nothing to do with what the paragraph is about.)
D. A concrete road is used only for heavy traffic.
   (This answer at least has something to do with the paragraph --
   concrete roads are used with heavy traffic but it does not say
   "used only.")
E. A concrete road is reinforced with other material.
   (This choice seems to be the correct one on two counts: *First*,
   the paragraph does suggest that concrete roads are made stronger
   by embedding steel bars in them. This is another way of saying
   "concrete roads are reinforced with steel bars." *Second*, by the
   process of elimination, the other four choices are ruled out as
   correct answers simply because they do not apply.)
You can be sure that not all the reading questions will be so easy
as these.

HINTS FOR ANSWERING READING QUESTIONS

1. Read the paragraph carefully. Then read each suggested answer carefully. Read every word, because often one word can make the difference between a right and a wrong answer.
2. Choose that answer which is supported in the paragraph itself. Do
   not choose an answer which is a correct statement unless it is based
   on information in the paragraph.
3. Even though a suggested answer has many of the words used in the
   paragraph, it may still be wrong.
4. Look out for words -- such as *always, never, entirely, or only* --
   which tend to make a suggested answer wrong.
5. Answer first those questions which you can answer most easily. Then
   work on the other questions.
6. If you can't figure out the answer to the question, guess.

EXAMINATION SECTION

DIRECTIONS FOR THIS SECTION:
  Each question has five suggested answers, lettered A to E. Decide
which one is the BEST answer. *PRINT THE LETTER OF THE CORRECT ANSWER
IN THE SPACE AT THE RIGHT.*

TEST 1

1. Some specialists are willing to give their services to the   1. ...
   Government entirely free of charge; some feel that a nominal
   salary, such as will cover traveling expenses, is sufficient
   for a position that is recognized as being somewhat honorary
   in nature; many other specialists value their time so highly
   that they will not devote any of it to public service that
   does not repay them at a rate commensurate with the fees that
   they can obtain from a good private clientele.
   *The paragraph BEST supports the statement that the use of
   specialists by the Government*
     A. is rare because of the high cost of securing such persons
     B. may be influenced by the willingness of specialists to
        serve
     C. enables them to secure higher salaries in private fields
     D. has become increasingly common during the past few years
     E. always conflicts with private demands for their services

2. The fact must not be overlooked that only about one-half of   2. ..
   the international trade of the world crosses the oceans. The
   other half is merely exchanges of merchandise between countries lying alongside each other or at least within the same
   continent.
   The paragraph BEST supports the statement that
      A. the most important part of any country's trade is trans-
         oceanic
      B. domestic trade is insignificant when compared with for-
         eign trade
      C. the exchange of goods between neighborhing countries is
         not considered international trade
      D. foreign commerce is not necessarily carried on by water
      E. about one-half of the trade of the world is international

3. Individual differences in mental traits assume importance in 3. ..
   fitting workers to jobs because such personal characteristics
   are persistent and are relatively little influenced by training and experience.
   *The paragraph BEST supports the statement that training and
   experience*
      A. are limited in their effectiveness in fitting workers
         to jobs
      B. do not increase a worker's fitness for a job
      C. have no effect upon a person's mental traits
      D. have relatively little effect upon the individual's
         chances for success
      E. should be based on the mental traits of an individual

4. The competition of buyers tends to keep prices up, the com-   4. ..
   petition of sellers to send them down. Normally the pressure
   of competition among sellers is stronger than that among buyers since the seller has his article to sell and must get rid
   of it, whereas the buyer is not committed to anything.
   *The paragraph BEST supports the statement that low prices
   are caused by*
      A. buyer competition
      B. competition of buyers with sellers
      C. fluctuations in demand
      D. greater competition among sellers than among buyers
      E. more sellers than buyers

5. In seventeen states, every lawyer is automatically a member 5. ..
   of the American Bar Association. In some other states and lo-
   calities, truly representative organizations of the Bar have
   not yet come into being, but are greatly needed.
   The paragraph IMPLIES that
      A. representative Bar Associations are necessary in states
         where they do not now exist
      B. every lawyer is required by law to become a member of
         the Bar
      C. the Bar Association is a democratic organization
      D. some states have more lawyers than others
      E. every member of the American Bar Association is automa-
         tically a lawyer in seventeen states.

TEST 2

1. We hear a great deal about the new education, and see a great 1. ...
deal of it in action. But the school house, though prodigious-
ly magnified in scale, is still very much the same old school
house.
The paragraph IMPLIES that
   A. the old education was, after all, better than the new
   B. although the modern school buildings are larger than
      the old ones, they have not changed very much in other
      respects
   C. the old school houses do not fit in with modern education-
      al theories
   D. a fine school building does not make up for poor teachers
   E. schools will be schools

2. No two human beings are of the same pattern --not even twins-- 2. ...
and the method of bringing out the best in each one necessar-
ily varies according to the nature of the child.
The paragraph IMPLIES that
   A. individual differences should be considered in dealing
      with children
   B. twins should be treated impartially
   C. it is an easy matter to determine the special abilities
      of children
   D. a child's nature varies from year to year
   E. we must discover the general technique of dealing with
      children

3. Man inhabits today a world very different from that which en- 3. ...
compassed even his parents and grandparents. It is a world
geared to modern machinery - automobiles, airplanes, power
plants; it is linked together and served by electricity.
The paragraph IMPLIES that
   A. the world has not changed much during the last few
      generations
   B. modern inventions and discoveries have brought about
      many changes in man's way of living
   C. the world is run more efficiently today than it was in
      our grandparents' time
   D. man is much happier today than he was a hundred years ago
   E. we must learn to see man as he truly is, underneath the
      veneers of man's contrivances

4. Success in any study depends largely upon the interest taken 4. ...
in that particular subject by the student. This being the case,
each teacher earnestly hopes that her students will realize at
the very outset that shorthand can be made an intensely fascina-
ting study.
The paragraph IMPLIES that
   A. everyone is interested in shorthand
   B. success in a study is entirely impossible unless the
      student finds the study very interesting
   C. if a student is eager to study shorthand, he is likely
      to succeed in it
   D. shorthand is necessary for success
   E. anyone who is not interested in shorthand will not suc-
      ceed in business

5. The primary purpose of all business English is to move the 5. ...
reader to agreeable and mutually profitable action. This action may be indirect or direct, but in either case a highly
competitive appeal for business should be clothed with inci-
sive diction tending to replace vagueness and doubt with clar-
ity, confidence, and appropriate action.
The paragraph IMPLIES that the
    A. ideal business letter uses words to conform to the read-
       er's language level
    B. business correspondent should strive for conciseness in
       letter writing
    C. keen competition of today has lessened the value of the
       letter as an appeal for business
    D. writer of a business letter should employ incisive dic-
       tion to move the reader to compliant and gainful action
    E. the writer of a business letter should be himself clear,
       confident, and forceful

TEST 3

1. To serve the community best, a comprehensive city plan must 1. ...
coordinate all physical improvements, even at the possible
expense of subordinating individual desires, to the end that
a city may grow in a more orderly way and provide adequate
facilities for its people.
The paragraph IMPLIES that
    A. city planning provides adequate facilities for recreation
    B. a comprehensive city plan provides the means for a city
       to grow in a more orderly fashion
    C. individual desires must always be subordinated to civic
       changes
    D. the only way to serve a community is to adopt a compre-
       hensive city plan
    E. city planning is the most important function of city
       government
2. Facility in writing letters, the knack of putting into these 2. ...
quickly written letters the same personal impression that
would mark an interview, and the ability to boil down to a
one-page letter the gist of what might be called a five or
ten minute conversation - all these are essential to effective
work under conditions of modern business organization.
The paragraph IMPLIES that
    A. letters are of more importance in modern business activi-
       ties than ever before
    B. letters should be used in place of interviews
    C. the ability to write good letters is essential to effec-
       tive work in modern business organization
    D. business letters should never be more than one page in
       length
    E. the person who can write a letter with great skill will
       get ahead more readily than others

3. The general rule is that it is the city council which deter-   3. ...
   mines the amount to be raised by taxation and which therefore
   determines, within the law, the tax rates. As has been pointed
   out, however, no city council or city authority has the power
   to determine what kinds of taxes should be levied.
   The paragraph IMPLIES that
      A. the city council has more authority than any other munici-
         pal body
      B. while the city council has a great deal of authority in
         the levying of taxes, its power is not absolute
      C. the kinds of taxes levied in different cities vary great-
         ly
      D. the city council appoints the tax collectors
      E. the mayor determines the kinds of taxes to be levied

4. The growth of modern business has made necessary mass produc-   4. ...
   tion, mass distribution, and mass selling. As a result, the
   problems of personnel and industrial relations have increased
   so rapidly that grave injustices in the handling of personal
   relationships have frequently occurred. Personnel administration is complex because, as in all human problems, many in-
   tangible elements are involved. Therefore a thorough, systema-
   tic, and continuous study of the psychology of human behavior
   is essential to the intelligent handling of personnel.
   The paragraph IMPLIES that
      A. complex modern industry makes impossible the personal re-
         lationships which formerly existed between employer and
         employee
      B. mass decisions are successfully applied to personnel
         problems
      C. the human element in personnel administration makes con-
         tinuous study necessary to its intelligent application
      D. personnel problems are less important than the problems
         of mass production and mass distribution
      E. since personnel administration is so complex and costly,
         it should be subordinated to the needs of good industrial
         relations

5. The Social Security Act is striving toward the attainment of   5. ...
   economic security for the individual and for his family. It was
   stated, in outlining this program, that security for the individual and for the family concerns itself with three factors:
   (1) decent homes to live in; (2) development of the natural resources of the country so as to afford the fullest opportunity
   to engage in productive work; and (3) safeguards against the major misfortunes of life. The Social Security Act is concerned
   with the third of these factors -"safeguards against misfortunes
   which cannot be wholly eliminated in this man-made world of ours."
   The paragraph IMPLIES that
      A. the Social Security Act is concerned primarily with supply-
         ing to families decent homes in which to live
      B. the development of natural resources is the only means of
         offering employment to the masses of the unemployed
      C. the Social Security Act has attained absolute economic
         security for the individual and for his family
      D. the Social Security Act deals with the first (1) factor
         as stated in the paragraph above
      E. the Social Security Act deals with the third (3) factor
         as stated in the paragraph above

TEST 4

Free unrhymed verse has been practiced for some thousands of years and reaches back to the incantation which linked verse with the ritual dance. It provided a communal emotion; the aim of the cadenced phrases was to create a state of mind. The general coloring of free rhythms in the poetry of today is that of speech rhythm, composed in the sequence of the musical phrase, not in the sequence of the metronome, the regular beat. In the twenties, conventional rhyme fell into almost complete disuse. This liberation from rhyme became as well a liberation of rhyme. Freed of its exacting task of supporting lame verse, it would be applied with greater effect where wanted for some special effect. Such break in the tradition of rhymed verse had the healthy effect of giving it a fresh start, released from the hampering convention of too familiar cadences. This refreshing and subtilizing of the use of rhyme can be seen everywhere in the poetry today.

1. The title below that BEST expresses the ideas of this para-   1. ...
   graph is:
   A. Primitive poetry
   B. The origin of poetry
   C. Rhyme and rhythm in modern verse
   D. Classification of poetry
   E. Purposes in all poetry
2. Free verse had its origin in primitive   2. ...
   A. fairy tales   B. literature   C. warfare   D. chants
   E. courtship
3. The object of early free verse was to   3. ...
   A. influence the mood of the people   B. convey ideas
   C. produce mental pictures   D. create pleasing sounds
   E. provide enjoyment

Control of the Mississippi had always been goals of nations having ambitions in the New World. La Salle claimed it for France in 1682. Iberville appropriated it to France when he colonized Louisiana in 1700. Bienville founded New Orleans, its principal port, as a French city in 1718. The fleur-de-lis were the blazon of the delta country until 1762. Then Spain claimed all of Louisiana. The Spanish were easy neighbors. American products from western Pennsylvania and the Northwest Territory were barged down the Ohio and Mississippi to New Orleans; here they were reloaded on ocean-going vessels that cleared for the great seaports of the world.

1. The title below that BEST expresses the ideas of this para-   1. ...
   graph is:
   A. Importance of seaports
   B. France and Spain in the New World
   C. Early control of the Mississippi
   D. Claims of European nations
   E. American trade on the Mississippi
2. Until 1762 the lower Mississippi area was held by   2. ...
   A. England   B. Spain   C. the United States
   D. France   E. Indians

3. In doing business with Americans the Spaniards were   3. ...
   A. easy to outsmart   B. friendly to trade
   C. inclined to charge high prices for use of their ports
   D. shrewd   E. suspicious

PASSAGE 3

Our humanity is by no means so materialistic as foolish talk is continually asserting it to be. Judging by what I have learned about men and women, I am convinced that there is far more in them of idealistic willpower than ever comes to the surface of the world. Just as the water of streams is small in amount compared to that which flows underground, so the idealism which becomes visible is small in amount compared with that which men and women bear locked in their hearts, unreleased or scarcely released. To unbind what is bound, to bring the underground waters to the surface -- mankind is waiting and longing for men who can do that.

1. The title below that BEST expresses the ideas of this para-   1. ...
   graph is:
   A. Releasing underground riches
   B. The good and bad in man
   C. Materialism in humanity
   D. The surface and the depths of idealism
   E. Unreleased energy
2. Human beings are more idealistic than   2. ...
   A. the water in underground streams
   B. their waiting and longing proves
   C. outward evidence shows
   D. the world
   E. other living creatures

PASSAGE 4

The total impression made by any work of fiction cannot be rightly understood without a sympathetic perception of the artistic aims of the writer. Consciously or unconsciouly, he has accepted certain facts, and rejected or suppressed other facts, in order to give unity to the particular aspect of human life which he is depicting. No novelist possesses the impartiality, the indifference, the infinite tolerance of nature. Nature displays to use, with complete unconcern, the beautiful and the ugly, the precious and the trivial, the pure and the impure. But a writer must select the aspects of nature and human nature which are demanded by the work in hand. He is forced to select, to combine, to create.

1. The title below that BEST expresses the ideas of this para-   1. ...
   graph is:
   A. Impressionists in literature
   B. Nature as an artist
   C. The novelist as an imitator
   D. Creative technic of the novelist
   E. Aspects of nature
2. A novelist rejects some facts because they   2. ...
   A. are impure and ugly
   B. would show he is not impartial
   C. are unrelated to human nature
   D. would make a bad impression
   E. mar the unity of his story

3. It is important for a reader to know   3. ..
    A. the purpose of the author
    B. what facts the author omits
    C. both the ugly and the beautiful
    D. something about nature
    E. what the author thinks of human nature

PASSAGE 5
If you watch a lamp which is turned very rapidly on and off, and y
keep your eyes open, "persistence of vision" will bridge the gaps of
darkness between the flashes of light, and the lamp will seem to be
continuously lit. This "topical afterglow" explains the magic produce
by the stroboscope, a new instrument which seems to freeze the swifte
motions while they are still going on, and to stop time itself dead i
its tracks. The "magic" is all in the eye of the beholder.

1. The "magic" of the stroboscope is due to   1. ..
    A. continuous lighting   B. intense cold
    C. slow motion   D. behavior of the human eye
    E. a lapse of time
2. "Persistence of vision" is explained by   2. ..
    A. darkness   B. winking   C. rapid flashes
    D. gaps   E. after impression

TEST 5
PASSAGE 1
During the past fourteen years, thousands of top-lofty United Stat
elms have been marked for death by the activities of the tiny Europea
elm bark beetle. The beetles, however, do not do fatal damage. Death
caused by another importation, Dutch elm disease, a fungus infection
which the beetles carry from tree to tree. Up to 1941, quarantine and
tree-sanitation measures kept the beetles and the disease pretty well
confined within 510 miles around metropolitan New York. War curtailed
these measures and made Dutch elm disease a wider menace. Every house
hold and village that prizes an elm-shaded lawn or commons must now
watch for it. Since there is as yet no cure for it, the infected tree
must be pruned or felled, and the wood must be burned in order to pro
tect other healthy trees.

1. The title below that BEST expresses the ideas of this para-   1. ..
    graph is:
        A. A menace to our elms   B. Pests and diseases of the elm
        C. Our vanishing elms   D. The need to protect Dutch elms
        E. How elms are protected
2. The danger of spreading the Dutch elm disease was increased   2. ..
    by
        A. destroying infected trees   B. the war
        C. the lack of a cure   D. a fungus infection
        E. quarantine measures
3. The European elm bark beetle is a serious threat to our elms 3. ..
    because it
        A. chews the bark   B. kills the trees
        C. is particularly active on the eastern seaboard
        D. carries infection   E. cannot be controlled

PASSAGE 2

It is elemental that the greater the development of man, the greater the problems he has to concern him. When he lived in a cave with stone implements, his mind no less than his actions was grooved into simple channels. Every new invention, every new way of doing things posed fresh problems for him. And, as he moved along the road, he questioned each step, as indeed he should, for he trod upon the beliefs of his ancestors. It is equally elemental to say that each step upon this later road posed more questions than the earlier ones. It is only the edcated man who realizes the results of his actions; it is only the thoughtful one who questions his own decisions.

1. The title below that BEST expresses the ideas of this paragraph is: 1. ...
    A. Channels of civilization
    B. The mark of a thoughtful man
    C. The cave man in contrast with man today
    D. The price of early progress
    E. Man's never-ending challenge

PASSAGE 3

Spring is one of those things that man has no hand in, any more than he has a part in sunrise or the phases of the moon. Spring came before man was here to enjoy it, and it will go right on coming even if man isn't here some time in the future. It is a matter of solar mechanics and celestial order. And for all our knowledge of astronomy and terrestrial mechanics, we haven't yet been able to do more than bounce a radar beam off the moon. We couldn't alter the arrival of the spring equinox by as much as one second, if we tried.

Spring is a matter of growth, of chlorophyll, of bud and blossom. We can alter growth and change the time of blossoming in individual plants; but the forests still grow in nature's way, and the grass of the plains hasn't altered its nature in a thousand years. Spring is a magnificent phase of the cycle of nature; but man really hasn't any guiding or controlling hand in it. He is here to enjoy it and benefit by it. And April is a good time to realize it; by May perhaps we will want to take full credit.

1. The title below that BEST expresses the ideas of this passage is: 1. ...
    A. The marvels of the Spring equinox
    B. Nature's dependence on mankind
    C. The weakness of man opposed to nature
    D. The glories of the world
    E. Eternal growth
2. The author of the passage states that   2. ...
    A. man has a part in the phases of the moon
    B. April is a time for taking full-credit
    C. April is a good time to enjoy nature
    D. man has a guiding hand in spring
    E. spring will cease to be if civilization ends

PASSAGE 4

The walled medieval town was as characteristic of its period as the cut of a robber baron's beard. It sprang out of the exigencies of war, and it was not without its architectural charm, whatever its hygienic deficiencies may have been. Behind its high, thick walls not only the normal inhabitants but the whole countryside fought and cowered in an hour of need. The capitals of Europe now forsake the city when the sirens scream and death from the sky seems imminent. Will the fear of bombs accelerate the slow decentralization which began with the automobile and the wide distribution of electrical energy and thus reverse the medieval flow to the city?

1. The title below that BEST expresses the ideas in this para-   1. ...
   graph is.
      A. A changing function of the town B. The walled medieval town
      C. The automobile's influence on city life D. Forsaking the city
      E. Bombs today and yesterday
2. Conditions in the Middle Ages made the walled town   2. ...
      A. a natural development   B. the most dangerous of all places
      C. a victim of fires   D. lacking in architectural charm
      E. healthful
3. Modern conditions may   3. ...
      A. make cities larger   B. make cities more hygienic
      C. protect against floods
      D. cause people to move from population centers
      E. encourage good architecture

PASSAGE 5

The literary history of this nation began when the first settler from abroad of sensitive mind paused in his adventure long enough to feel that he was under a different sky, breathing new air, and that a New World was all before him with only his strength and Providence for guides. With him began a new emphasis upon an old theme in literature, the theme of cutting loose and faring forth, renewed, under the powerful influence of a fresh continent for civilized man. It has provided, ever since those first days, a strong current in our native literature, whose other flow has come from a nostalgia for the rich culture of Europe, so much of which was perforce left behind.

1. The title below that BEST expresses the ideas of this para-   1. ...
   graph is:
      A. America's distinctive literature B. Pioneer authors
      C. The dead hand of the past D. Europe's literary grandchild
      E. America comes of age
2. American writers, according to the author, because of their   2. ...
   colonial experiences
      A. were antagonistic to European writers
      B. cut loose from Old World influences
      C. wrote only on New World events and characters
      D. created new literary themes
      E. gave fresh interpretation to an old literary idea

TEST 6

1. Any business not provided with capable substitutes to fill 1. ...
all important positions is a weak business. Therefore a fore-
man should train each man not only to perform his own parti-
cular duties but also to do those of two or three positions.
The paragraph BEST supports the statement that
   A. dependence on substitutes is a sign of weak organization
   B. training will improve the strongest organization
   C. the foreman should be the most expert at any particular
      job under him
   D. every employee can be trained to perform efficiently
      work other than his own
   E. vacancies in vital positions should be provided for in
      advance

2. The coloration of textile fabrics composed of cotton and 2. ...
wool generally requires two processes, as the process used
in dyeing wool is seldom capable of fixing the color upon
cotton. The usual method is to immerse the fabric in the re-
quisite baths to dye the wool and then to treat the partially dyed material in the manner found suitable for cotton.
The paragraph BEST supports the statement that the dyeing
of textile fabrics composed of cotton and wool
   A. is less complicated than the dyeing of wool alone
   B. is more successful when the material contains more
      cotton than wool
   C. is not satisfactory when solid colors are desired
   D. is restricted to two colors for any one fabric
   E. is usually based upon the methods required for dyeing
      the different materials

3. The serious investigator must direct his whole effort toward 3. ...
success in his work. If he wishes to succeed in each inves-
tigation, his work will be by no means easy, smooth, or peace-
ful; on the contrary, he will have to devote himself complete-
ly and continuously to a task that requires all his ability.
The paragraph BEST supports the statement that an investiga-
tor's success depends most upon
   A. ambition to advance rapidly in the service
   B. persistence in the face of difficulty
   C. training and experience
   D. willingness to obey orders without delay
   E. the number of investigations which he conducts

4. Honest people in one nation find it difficult to understand 4. ...
the viewpoint of honest people in another. State departments
and their ministers exist for the purpose of explaining the
viewpoints of one nation in terms understood by another. Some
of their most important work lies in this direction.
The paragraph BEST supports the statement that
   A. people of different nations may not consider matters
      in the same light
   B. it is unusual for many people to share similar ideas
   C. suspicion prevents understanding between nations
   D. the chief work of state departments is to guide rela-
      tions between nations united by a common cause
   E. the people of one nation must sympathize with the view-
      points of others

13

5. Economy once in a while is just not enough. I expect to find 5. ...
it at every level of responsibility, from cabinet member to
the newest and youngest recruit. Controlling waste is some-
thing like bailing a boat; you have to keep at it. I have no
intention of easing up on my insistence on getting a dollar
of value for each dollar we spend.
The paragraph BEST supports the statement that
   A. we need not be concerned about items which cost less
      than a dollar
   B. it is advisable to buy the cheaper of two items
   C. the responsibility of economy is greater at high levels
      than at low levels
   D. economy becomes easy with practice
   E. economy is a continuing responsibility

TEST 7

1. On all permit imprint mail the charge for postage has been   1. ...
printed by the mailer before he presents it for mailing and
pays the postage. Such mail of any class is mailable only at
the post office that issued a permit covering it. Since the
postage receipts for such mail represent only the amount of
permit imprint mail detected and verified, employees in re-
ceiving, handling, and outgoing sections must be alert constantly to route such mail to the weighing section before it
is handled or dispatched.
The paragraph BEST supports the statement that, at post of-
fices where permit mail is received for dispatch,
   A. dispatching units make a final check on the amount of
      postage payable on permit imprint mail
   B. employees are to check the postage chargeable on mail
      received under permit
   C. neither more nor less postage is to be collected than
      the amount printed on permit imprint mail
   D. the weighing section is primarily responsible for fail-
      ure to collect postage on such mail
   E. unusual measures are taken to prevent unstamped mail
      from being accepted

2. Education should not stop when the individual has been pre-   2. ...
pared to make a livelihood and to live in modern society.
Living would be mere existence were there no appreciation
and enjoyment of the riches of art, literature, and science.
The paragraph BEST supports the statement that true education
   A. is focused on the routine problems of life
   B. prepares one for full enjoyment of life
   C. deals chiefly with art, literature and science
   D. is not possible for one who does not enjoy scientific
      literature
   E. disregards practical ends

3. Insured and c.o.d. air and surface mail is accepted with   3. ...
the understanding that the sender guarantees any necessary
forwarding or return postage. When such mail is forwarded or
returned, it shall be rated up for collection of postage; except that insured or c.o.d. air mail weighing 8 ounces or less

and subject to the 10 cents an ounce rate shall be forwarded by air if delivery will be advanced, and returned by surface means, without additional postage.

The paragraph BEST supports the statement that the return postage for undeliverable insured mail is
- A. included in the original prepayment on air mail parcels
- B. computed but not collected before dispatching surface patrol post mail to sender
- C. not computed or charged for any air mail that is returned by surface transportation
- D. included in the amount collected when the sender mails parcel post
- E. collected before dispatching for return if any amount due has been guaranteed

4. All undeliverable first-class mail, except first-class parcels and parcel post paid with first-class postage, which cannot be returned to the sender, is sent to a dead-letter branch. Undeliverable matter of the third-and fourth-classes of obvious value for which the sender does not furnish return postage and undeliverable first-class parcels and parcel-post matter bearing postage of the first-class, which cannot be returned, is sent to a dead parcel-post branch.   4. ...

The paragraph BEST supports the statement that matter that is sent to a dead parcel-post branch includes all undeliverable
- A. mail, except first-class letter mail, that appears to be valuable
- B. mail, except that of the first-class, on which the sender failed to prepay the original mailing costs
- C. parcels on which the mailer prepaid the first-class rate of postage
- D. third- and fourth-class matter on which the required return postage has not been paid
- E. parcels on which first-class postage has been prepaid, when the sender's address is not known

5. Civilization started to move rapidly when man freed himself of the shackles that restricted his search for truth.   5. ...

The paragraph BEST supports the statement that the progress of civilization
- A. came as a result of man's dislike for obstacles
- B. did not begin until restrictions on learning were removed
- C. has been aided by man's efforts to find the truth
- D. is based on continually increasing efforts
- E. continues at a constantly increasing rate

TEST 8

1. Telegrams should be clear, concise, and brief. Omit all un-   1. ... necessary words. The parts of speech most often used in telegrams are nouns, verbs, adjectives, and adverbs. If possible, do without pronouns, prepositions, articles, and copulative verbs. Use simple sentences, rather than complex and compound.

The paragraph BEST supports the statement that in writing telegrams one should always use
- A. common and simple words

    B. only nouns,verbs,adjectives,and adverbs
    C. incomplete sentences
    D. only words essential to the meaning
    E. the present tense of verbs
2. The function of business is to increase the wealth of the   2. ...
   country and the value and happiness of life. It does this
   by supplying the material needs of men and women. When the
   nation's business is successfully carried on, it renders
   public service of the highest value.
   The paragraph BEST supports the statement that
    A. all businesses which render public service are success-
       ful
    B. human happiness is enhanced only by the increase of ma-
       terial wants
    C. the value of life is increased only by the increase of
       wealth
    D. the material needs of men and women are supplied by well-
       conducted business
    E. business is the only field of activity which increases
       happiness
3. In almost every community, fortunately, there are certain   3. ...
   men and women known to be public-spirited. Others, however,
   may be selfish and act only as their private interests seem
   to require.
   The paragraph BEST supports the statement that those citizens
   who disregard others are
    A. fortunate   B. needed
    C. found only in small communities   D. not known
    E. not public-spirited

KEY (CORRECT ANSWERS)

TEST 1	TEST 4	TEST 5	TEST 6
1. B	PASSAGE 1	PASSAGE 1	1. E
2. D	1. C	1. A	2. E
3. A	2. D	2. B	3. B
4. D	3. A	3. D	4. A
5. A	PASSAGE 2	PASSAGE 2	5. E
	1. C	1. E	
TEST 2	2. D	PASSAGE 3	TEST 7
1. B	3. B	1. C	1. B
2. A	PASSAGE 3	2. C	2. B
3. B	1. D	PASSAGE 4	3. B
4. C	2. C	1. A	4. E
5. D	PASSAGE 4	2. A	5. C
	1. D	3. D	
TEST 3	2. E	PASSAGE 5	TEST 8
1. B	2. A	1. A	1. D
2. C	PASSAGE 5	2. E	2. D
3. B	1. D		3. E
4. C	2. E		
5. E			

Basic Mathematics
EXAMINATION SECTION

DIRECTIONS: Each question or incomplete statement is followed by several suggested answers or completions. Select the one that BEST answers the question or completes the statement. *PRINT THE LETTER OF THE CORRECT ANSWER IN THE SPACE AT THE RIGHT.*

1. 534
    18
    +1291

    A. 1733   B. 1743   C. 1833   D. 1843   E. 1853   1.____

2. $(17 \times 23) - 16 + 20 =$
    A. 459   B. 427   C. 411   D. 395   E. 355   2.____

3. $3/7 + 5/11 =$
    A. 33/35   B. 4/9   C. 8/18   D. 68/77   E. 15/77   3.____

4. $4832 \div 6 =$
    A. 905 1/3   B. 805 1/3   C. 95 1/3   D. 95   E. 85 1/3   4.____

5. $62.3 - 4.9 =$
    A. 5.74   B. 7.4   C. 57.4   D. 58.4   E. 67.4   5.____

6. $3/5 \times 4/9 =$
    A. 4/15   B. 7/45   C. 27/20   D. 12/14   E. 15/4   6.____

7. $14/16 - 5/16 =$
    A. 8/16   B. 9/16   C. 11/16   D. 8   E. 9   7.____

8. $5.03 + 2.7 + 40 =$
    A. .570   B. 4.773   C. 5.70   D. 11.73   E. 47.73   8.____

9. $5.37 \times 21.4 =$
    A. 11491.8   B. 1149.18   C. 114.918   D. 11.4918   E. 1.14918   9.____

10. $5 \ 1/4 + 2 \ 7/8 =$
    A. $8\frac{1}{4}$ B. 8 1/8   C. 7 2/3   D. $7\frac{1}{4}$ E. 7 1/8   10.____

11. $-14 + 5 =$
    A. -19   B. -9   C. 9   D. 19   E. 70   11.____

12. $2/7$ of $28 =$
    A. 98   B. 16   C. 14   D. 8   E. 4   12.____

13. $2/5 =$
    A. .10   B. .20   C. .25   D. .40   E. .52   13.____

14. 20% of _____ is 38.
    A. 7.6   B. 19   C. 76   D. 190   E. 760   14.____

15. $\dfrac{8.4}{400} =$

    A. .0021   B. .021   C. .21   D. 2.1   E. 21

15.___

16. $\dfrac{4}{5} = \dfrac{?}{60}$

    A. 240   B. 48   C. 20   D. 15   E. 12

16.___

17. What is the area of the rectangle shown at the right?
    A. 47 mm^2
    B. 94 mm^2
    C. 240 mm^2
    D. 480 mm^2
    E. 960 mm^2

17.___

18. What number does ☐ represent in this equation?

    $25 - ☐ - ☐ - ☐ - ☐ = 13$

    A. 13   B. 12   C. 7   D. 4   E. 3

18.___

19. Approximate lengths are given in the right triangles shown at the right.
What does length x equal?
    A. 48
    B. 39
    C. 37
    D. 35
    E. 32

19.___

20. What is the perimeter of the triangle shown at the right?
    A. 10 × 15 × 17
    B. 10 + 15 + 17
    C. ½ × 10 × 15
    D. ½ × 10 × 17
    E. ½(10 + 15 + 17)

20.___

21. Which of the following expressions will give the same answer as 45 × 9?
    A. 5 × 3^3 B. (4×9) + (5×9)
    C. (40+9) × 5   D. (45×3) + (45×3)
    E. (45×10) - (45×1)

21.___

22. Find the average of 19, 21, 21, 22, and 27.
    A. 23   B. 22   C. 21   D. 20   E. 19

22.___

23. In the triangle at the right, how many
    degrees is ∠T?
    A. 75°
    B. 85°
    C. 95°
    D. 115°
    E. 180°

23.___

24.

24.___

About how long is the paper clip?
    A. 5 cm   B. 4 cm   C. 3 cm   D. 2 cm   E. 1 cm

25. Five stores sell the same size cans of tomato soup. Their
    prices are listed below.
    Which sells the soup for the LOWEST price per can?
    _____ cans for _____.
    A. 6; 99¢   B. 6; 90¢   C. 5; 93¢   D. 3; 56¢   E. 3; 50¢

25.___

26. Rock star Peter Giles receives $1.97 royalty on each of his
    albums that is sold. 14,127 albums are sold.
    Estimate how much Peter Giles will receive.
    A. $7,000   B. $14,000   C. $20,000   D. $26,000   E. $28,000

26.___

27. An amplifier is advertised for 20% off the list price of
    $430.
    What is the sale price?
    A. $516   B. $454   C. $354   D. $344   E. $215

27.___

28. If 9 dozen eggs cost $3.60, what do 25 dozen eggs cost?
    A. $90.00   B. $10.00   C. $9.00   D. $2.54   E. $.40

28.___

29. The distance between New York and San Antonio is 1860 miles.
    If a jet averages 465 miles per hour, how many hours will
    it take to travel the distance?
    A. 9   B. 5   C. 4   D. 3   E. 2

29.___

30. In a high school homeroom of 32 students, 24 are girls.
    What percent are girls?
    A. 3/4%   B. 24%   C. 25%   D. 75%   E. 80%

30.___

31. Which problem could give the answer shown
    on the calculator?
    A. 2 + .3
    B. 2 × 3/10
    C. 2 × 1/3
    D. 33333 + .2
    E. 7 ÷ 3

31. ___

```
┌─────────────┐
│  2 .33333   │
└─────────────┘
  ┌─┐┌─┐┌─┐┌─┐
  │7││8││9││+│
  └─┘└─┘└─┘└─┘
  ┌─┐┌─┐┌─┐┌─┐
  │4││5││6││−│
  └─┘└─┘└─┘└─┘
  ┌─┐┌─┐┌─┐┌─┐
  │1││2││3││x│
  └─┘└─┘└─┘└─┘
  ┌─┐┌─┐┌─┐┌─┐
  │0││·││=││÷│
  └─┘└─┘└─┘└─┘
```

32. According to the table at the
    right, how much will it cost in
    a typical week for the 3 members
    of the Wright family to eat at
    home? Mr. Wright is 56 years old;
    Mrs. Wright, 52; and their son
    Harry, 17.
    A. $125
    B. $52
    C. $49
    D. $42
    E. $40

32. ___

Cost of Eating at Home
(one week)

Age	Male	Female
6-11 yrs.	$14	$14
12-19 yrs.	$19	$16
20-54 yrs.	$20	$16
55 and up	$14	$14

33. According to the table shown in the previous question, how
    much does it cost in a typical four-week month to feed a
    12-year-old girl?
    A. $4   B. $16   C. $48   D. $64   E. $78

33. ___

34. Reverend Wilhite jogs for 1½ hours each day, 6 days a week.
    If he burns 800 calories per hour of jogging, how many
    calories does he burn in a week?
    A. 4800   B. 5600   C. 7200   D. 8400   E. 9000

34. ___

35. Ground meat costs 90¢ per pound.
    How much does the meat on the scale
    cost?
    A. $1.80
    B. $1.60
    C. $1.54
    D. $1.44
    E. $.90

35. ___

36. According to the graph at the
    right, about when did the
    weekly wages for a minimum
    wage worker go over $100?
    A. 1965
    B. 1970
    C. 1975
    D. 1979
    E. 1980

36. ___

Weekly Wages for a Minimum-Wage Employee

37. According to the bar graph at the right, what is the approximate height of the Crystal Beach Comet?
    A. 40 ft.
    B. 90 ft.
    C. 92 ft.
    D. 94 ft.
    E. 98 ft.

Heights of Great Roller Coasters

37.____

38. According to the bar graph shown in the previous question, what is the difference in height between the tallest and shortest roller coasters?
    ____ feet.
    A. 5   B. 10   C. 15   D. 20   E. 50

38.____

39. How much change will you receive from a $10 bill when you buy 4 grapefruits at 90¢ each and 3 apples at 40¢ each?
    A. $6.20   B. $5.20   C. $4.80   D. $4.20   E. $4.00

39.____

40. A medical supplier packages medicine in boxes. The cost of packaging is computed with the flow chart at the right.
    What is the cost of packaging medicine in a box that is 30 cm long, 20 cm wide, and 20 cm high?
    A. $.20
    B. $.24
    C. $2.00
    D. $2.40
    E. $3.00

40.____

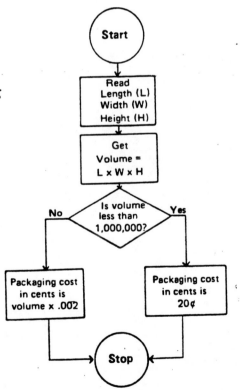

KEY (CORRECT ANSWERS)

1. D	11. B	21. E	31. E
2. D	12. D	22. B	32. C
3. D	13. D	23. B	33. D
4. B	14. D	24. C	34. C
5. C	15. B	25. B	35. D
6. A	16. B	26. E	36. C
7. B	17. D	27. D	37. D
8. E	18. E	28. B	38. C
9. C	19. A	29. C	39. B
10. B	20. B	30. D	40. A

SOLUTIONS TO PROBLEMS

1. $534 + 18 + 1291 = 1843$

2. $(17 \times 23) - 16 + 20 = 391 - 16 + 20 = 395$

3. $\frac{3}{7} + \frac{5}{11} = \frac{33}{77} + \frac{35}{77} = \frac{68}{77}$

4. $4832 \div 6 = 805 \frac{1}{3}$

5. $62.3 - 4.9 = 57.4$

6. $\frac{3}{5} \times \frac{4}{9} = \frac{12}{45} = \frac{4}{15}$

7. $\frac{14}{16} - \frac{5}{16} = \frac{9}{16}$

8. $5.03 + 2.7 + 40 = 47.73$

9. $5.37 \times 21.4 = 114.918$

10. $5\frac{1}{4} + 2\frac{7}{8} = 7\frac{9}{8} = 8\frac{1}{8}$

11. $-14 + 5 = -9$

12. $\frac{2}{7}$ of $28 = (\frac{2}{7})(\frac{28}{1}) = 8$

13. $\frac{2}{5} = .40$ as a decimal

14. Let x = missing number. Then, $.20x = 38$. Solving, $x = 190$

15. $\frac{8.4}{400} = .021$

16. Let x = missing number. Then, $\frac{4}{5} = \frac{x}{60}$. $5x = 240$, so $x = 48$

17. Area $= (15)(32) = 480 \text{mm}^2$

18. Let x = ☐. Then, $25 - 4x = 13$. So, $-4x = -12$. Solving, $x = 3$

19. $\frac{9}{27} = \frac{16}{x}$. Then, 9x = 432. Solving, x = 48.

20. Perimeter = 17 + 10 + 15 = 42

21. 45 × 9 = 405 = (45×10) - (45×1)

22. 19 + 21 + 21 + 22 + 27 = 110. Then, 110 ÷ 5 = 22

23. ∠T = 180° - 50° - 45° = 85°

24. The paper clip's length is about 5 - 2 = 3 cm.

25. For A: price per can = $\frac{.99}{6}$ = .165;

    For B: price per can = $\frac{.90}{6}$ = .15

    For C: price per can = $\frac{.93}{5}$ = .186

    For D: price per can = $\frac{.56}{3}$ = .18$\overline{6}$

    For E: price per can = $\frac{.50}{3}$ = .1$\overline{6}$

    Lowest price is for B.

26. \$1.97 ≈ \$2.00. Then, (\$2.00)(14,127) = \$28,254 ≈ \$28,000.

27. Sale price = (\$430)(.80) = \$344

28. Let x = cost. Then, $\frac{9}{360} = \frac{25}{x}$. 9x = \$90, so x = \$10.00

29. $\frac{1860}{465}$ = 4 hours

30. $\frac{24}{32}$ = 75%

31. $\frac{7}{3}$ = 2.$\overline{3}$ = 2.33333 on this calculator shown.

32. Total cost = \$14 + \$16 + \$19 = \$49

33. Cost = (\$16)(4) = \$64

34. (800)(1$\frac{1}{2}$)(6) = 7200 calories

35. (.90)(1.6) = \$1.44

36. Around 1975, the minimum weekly wages exceeded \$100.

37. The Crystal Beach Comet's height is about 94 ft.

38. Tallest ≈ 105 ft. and the shortest ≈ 90 ft.
    Difference = 15 ft.

39. $10 – (4)(.90) – (3)(.40) = $5.20 change

40. (30)(20)(20) = 12,000 cm^3. Since 12,000 < 1,000,000, the
    price is 20 cents.

EXAMINATION SECTION
TEST 1

DIRECTIONS: Each question or incomplete statement is followed by several suggested answers or completions. Select the one that BEST answers the question or completes the statement. *PRINT THE LETTER OF THE CORRECT ANSWER IN THE SPACE AT THE RIGHT.*

1. Which of the following fractions is the SMALLEST?

   A. $\frac{2}{3}$ B. $\frac{4}{5}$ C. $\frac{5}{7}$ D. $\frac{5}{11}$

   1.____

2. 40% is equivalent to which of the following?

   A. $\frac{4}{5}$ B. $\frac{4}{6}$ C. $\frac{2}{5}$ D. $\frac{4}{100}$

   2.____

3. How many 100's are in 10,000?

   A. 10   B. 100   C. 10,000   D. 100,000

   3.____

4. $\frac{6}{7} + \frac{11}{12}$ is approximately

   A. 1   B. 2   C. 17   D. 19

   4.____

5. The time required to heat water to a certain temperature is directly proportional to the volume of water being heated.
   If it takes 12 minutes to heat $1\frac{1}{2}$ gallons of water, how many minutes will it take to heat 2 gallons of water?

   A. 12   B. 16   C. 18   D. 24

   5.____

6. The cost of an item increased by 25%.
   If the original cost was C dollars, identify the expression which gives the new cost of that item.

   A. C + 0.25   B. $\frac{1}{4}$C   D. 25C   D. 1.25C

   6.____

7. Given the formula PV = nRT, all of the following are true EXCEPT

   A. $T = \frac{PV}{nR}$ B. $P = \frac{nRT}{V}$ C. $V = \frac{P}{nRT}$ D. $n = \frac{PV}{RT}$

   7.____

8. If a Fahrenheit (F) temperature reading is 104, find its Celsius (C) equivalent, given that $C = \frac{5}{9}(F-32)$

   A. 36   B. 40   C. 72   D. 76

   8.____

9. If 40% of a graduating class plans to go directly to work after graduation, which of the following must be TRUE?
   A. Less than half of the class plans to go directly to work.
   B. Forty members of the class plan to enter the job market.
   C. Most of the class plans to go directly to work.
   D. Six in ten members of the class are expected not to graduate.

   9.____

10. Given a multiple-choice test item which has 5 choices,   10.___
what is the probability of guessing the correct answer
if you know nothing about the item content?
    A. 5%   B. 10%   C. 20%   D. 25%

11. Which graph BEST represents the data
shown in the table at the right?

S	T
0	80
5	75
10	65
15	50
20	30
25	5

11.___

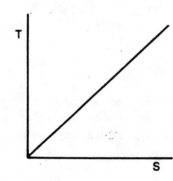

A.   C.

B.   D.

12. If $3(X + 5Y) = 24$, find Y when $X = 3$.   12.___

    A. 1   B. 3   C. $\frac{33}{5}$ D. 7

13. The payroll of a grocery store for its 23 clerks is   13.___
$395,421.
Which expression below shows the average salary of a
clerk?
    A. 395,421 × 23   B. 23 ÷ 395,421
    C. (395,421 × 14) ÷ 23   D. 395,421 ÷ 23

14. If 12.8 pounds of coffee cost $50.80, what is the   14.___
APPROXIMATE price per pound?
    A. $2.00   B. $3.00   C. $4.00   D. $5.00

15. A road map has a scale where 1 inch corresponds to 150   15.___
miles.
A distance of $3\frac{3}{4}$ inches on the map corresponds to what
actual distance?
    _____ miles
    A. 153.75   B. 375   C. 525   D. 562.5

16. How many square feet of plywood are
needed to construct the back and
4 adjacent sides of the box shown
at the right?
_____ square feet.
    A. 63
    B. 90
    C. 96
    D. 126

16._____

BACK

3 ft.

6 ft.

5 ft.

17. One thirty pound bag of lawn fertilizer costs $20.00 and
will cover 600 square feet of lawn. Terry's lawn is a
96 foot by 75 foot rectangle. How much will it cost Terry
to buy enough bags of fertilizer for her lawn?
Which of the following do you NOT need in order to solve
this problem?
The
    A. product of 96 and 75
    B. fact that one bag weighs 30 pounds
    C. fact that one bag covers 600 square feet
    D. fact that one bag costs $20.00

17._____

18. On the graph shown
at the right, between
which hours was the
drop in temperature
GREATEST?
    A. 11:00 - Noon
    B. Noon - 1:00
    C. 1:00 - 2:00
    D. 2:00 - 3:00

18._____

TEMPERATURE

30
25
20
15
10

11 00 Noon 1 00 2 00 3 00 4 00
Time

19. If on a typical railroad track, the distance from the
center of one railroad tie to the next is 30 inches,
approximately how many ties would be needed for one mile
of track?
    A. 180   B. 2,110   C. 6,340   D. 63,360

19._____

20. Which of the following is MOST likely to be the volume
of a wine bottle?
    A. 750 milliliters   B. 7 kilograms
    C. 7 milligrams   D. 7 liters

20._____

21. What is the reading on the gauge shown at the right?
    A. -7
    B. -3
    C. 1
    D. 3

21.____

22. Which statement below disproves the assertion, *All students in Mrs. Marino's 10th grade geometry class are planning to go to college?*
    A. Albert is in Mrs. Marino's class, but he is not planning to take mathematics next year.
    B. Jorge is not in Mrs. Marino's class, but he is still planning to go to college.
    C. Pierre is in Mrs. Marino's class but says he will not be attending school anymore after this year.
    D. Crystal is in Mrs. Marino's class and plans to attend Yale University when she graduates.

22.____

23. A store advertisement reads, *Buy now while our prices are low There will never be a better time to buy.* The customer reading this advertisement should assume that
    A. the prices at the store will probably never be lower
    B. right now, this store has the best prices in town
    C. prices are higher at other stores
    D. prices are always lowest at this store

23.____

24. *Given any positive integer A, there is always a positive number B such that A × B is less than 1.* Which statement below supports this generalization?

    A. $8 \times \frac{1}{16} = \frac{1}{2}$ B. $8 \times \frac{1}{2} = 4$

    C. $\frac{5}{2} \times \frac{1}{10} = \frac{1}{4}$ D. $\frac{1}{2} \times \frac{1}{2} = \frac{1}{4}$

24.____

25. Of the following expressions, which is equivalent to $4C + D = 12E$?
    A. $C = 4(12E - D)$ B. $4 + D = 12E - C$

    C. $4C + 12E = -D$ D. $C = \frac{12E-D}{4}$

25.____

KEY (CORRECT ANSWERS)

1. D
2. C
3. B
4. B
5. B

6. D
7. C
8. B
9. A
10. C

11. A
12. A
13. D
14. C
15. D

16. C
17. B
18. D
19. B
20. A

21. B
22. C
23. A
24. A
25. D

SOLUTIONS TO PROBLEMS

1. Converting to decimals, we get $.\overline{6}$, $.8$, $.714$ (approx), $.\overline{45}$. The smallest is $.\overline{45}$ corresponding to 5/11.

2. $40\% = 40/100 = \dfrac{2}{5}$

3. $10,000 \div 100 = 100$

4. $\dfrac{6}{7} + \dfrac{11}{12} = (72 + 77) \div 84 = \dfrac{149}{84} \approx 1.77 \approx 2$

5. Let x = required minutes. Then, $12/1\frac{1}{2} = x/2$
   This reduces to $1\frac{1}{2}x = 24$. Solving, $x = 16$

6. New cost is $C + .25C = 1.25C$

7. For $PV = nRT$, $V = nRT/P$

8. $C = \dfrac{5}{9}(104-32) = \dfrac{5}{9}(72) = 40$

9. Since 40% is less than 50% (or half), we conclude that less than half of the class plans to go to work directly after graduation.

10. The probability of guessing right is $\dfrac{1}{5}$ or 20%.

11. Curve A is most accurate since as S increases, we see that T decreases. Note, however, that the relationship is NOT linear. Although S increases in equal amounts, the decrease in T is NOT in equal amounts.

12. $3(3+5Y) = 24$. This simplifies to $9 + 15Y = 24$
    Solving, $Y = 1$

13. The average salary is $\$395,421 \div 23$

14. The price per pound is $\$50.80 \div 12.8 = \$3.96875$ or approximately $4.

15. Actual distance is $(3\frac{3}{4})(150) = 562.5$ miles

16. The area of the back = (6)(5) = 30 sq.ft. The combined area of the two vertical sides is (2)(6)(3) = 36 sq.ft. The combined area of the horizontal sides is (2)(5)(3) = 30 sq.ft. Total area = 30 + 36 + 30 = 96 square feet.

17. Choice B is not relevant to solving the problem since the cost will be [(96)(75) ÷ 600][$20] = $240. So, the weight per bag is not needed.

18. For the graph, the largest temperature drop was from 2:00 P.M. to 3:00 P.M. The temperature dropped 20 - 10 = 10 degrees.

19. 1 mile = 5280 feet = 63,360 inches. Then, 63,360 ÷ 30 = 2112 or about 2110 ties are needed.

20. Since 1 liter = 1.06 quarts, 750 milliliters = $(\frac{750}{1000})(1.06)$ = .795 quarts. This is a reasonable volume for a wine bottle.

21. The reading is -3.

22. Statement C contradicts the given information, since Pierre is in Mrs. Marino's class. Then he should plan to go to college.

23. Since there will never be a better time to buy at this particular store, the customer can assume the current prices will probably never be lower.

24. Statement A illustrates this concept. Note that in general, if n is a positive integer, then $(n)(\frac{1}{n+1}) < 1$

Example: $(100)(\frac{1}{101}) < 1$

TEST 2

DIRECTIONS: Each question or incomplete statement is followed by several suggested answers or completions. Select the one that BEST answers the question or completes the statement. *PRINT THE LETTER OF THE CORRECT ANSWER IN THE SPACE AT THE RIGHT.*

1. Which of the following lists numbers in INCREASING order?   1.___
   A. 0.4, 0.04, 0.004   B. 2.71, 3.15, 2.996
   C. 0.7, 0.77, 0.777   D. 0.06, 0.5, 0.073

2. $\frac{4}{10} + \frac{7}{100} + \frac{5}{1000} =$ 2.___

   A. 4.75   B. 0.475   C. 0.0475   D. 0.00475

3. 700 times what number equals 7?   3.___
   A. 10   B. 0.1   C. 0.01   D. 0.001

4. 943 – 251 is approximately   4.___
   A. 600   B. 650   C. 700   D. 1200

5. The time needed to set up a complicated piece of   5.___
   machinery is inversely proportional to the number of
   years' experience of the worker.
   If a worker with 10 years' experience needs 6 hours to
   do the job, how long will it take a worker with 15 years'
   experience?
   A. 4   B. 5   C. 9   D. 25

6. Let W represent the number of waiters and D, the number   6.___
   of diners in a particular restaurant.
   Identify the expression which represents the statement:
   There are 10 times as many diners as waiters.
   A. 10W = D   B. 10D = W
   C. 10D + 10W   D. 10 = D + W

7. Which of the following is equivalent to the formula   7.___
   F = XC + Y?
   A. F – C = X + Y   B. Y = F + XC

   C. $C = \frac{F\ Y}{X}$ D. $C = \frac{F\ X}{Y}$

8. Given the formula $A = \frac{BC}{D}$, if A = 12, B = 6, and D = 3,   8.___
   what is the value of C?
   A. $\frac{2}{3}$ B. 6   C. 18   D. 24

9. 5 is to 7 as X is to 35.
   X =
   A. 7   B. 12   C. 25   D. 49

   9.____

10. Kramer Middle School has 5 seventh grade mathematics teachers: two of the math teachers are women and three are men.
    If you are assigned a teacher at random, what is the probability of getting a female teacher?
    A. 0.2   B. 0.4   C. 0.6   D. 0.8

    10.____

11. Which statement BEST describes the graph shown at the right?
    Temperature
    A. and time decrease at the same rate
    B. and time increase at the same rate
    C. increases over time
    D. decreases over time

    11.____

12. If 3X + 4 = 2Y, find Y when X = 2.
    A. 0   B. 3   C. 4½   D. 5

    12.____

13. A car goes 243 miles on 8.7 gallons of gas.
    Which numeric expression should be used to determine the car's miles per gallon?
    A. 243 × 87   B. 8.7 ÷ 243
    C. 243 ÷ 8.7   D. 243 − 8.7

    13.____

14. What is the average cost per book if you buy six books at $4.00 each and four books at $5.00 each?
    A. $4.40   B. $4.50   C. $4.60   D. $5.40

    14.____

15. A publisher's sale offers a 15% discount to anyone buying more than 100 workbooks.
    What will be the discount on 200 workbooks selling at $2.25 each?
    A. $15.00   B. $30.00   C. $33.75   D. $67.50

    15.____

16. A road crew erects 125 meters of fencing in one workday.
    How many workdays are required to erect a kilometer of fencing?
    A. 0.8   B. 8   C. 80   D. 800

    16.____

17. Last month Kim made several telephone calls to New York   17.___
    City totaling 45 minutes in all.
    What does Kim need in order to calculate the average
    duration of her New York City calls?
    The
       A. total number of calls she made to New York City
       B. cost per minute of a call to New York City
       C. total cost of her telephone bill last month
       D. days of the week on which the calls were made

18.   18.___

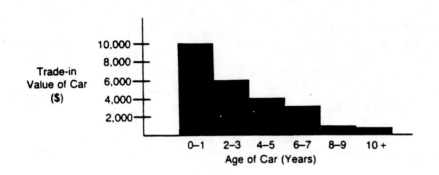

    The chart above relates a car's age to its trade-in value.
    Based on the chart, which of the following is TRUE?
       A. A 4- to 5-year old car has a trade-in value of about
          $2,000.
       B. The trade-in value of an 8- to 9-year old car is about
          1/3 that of a 2- to 3-year old car.
       C. A 6- to 7-year old car has no trade-in value.
       D. A 4- to 5-year old car's trade-in value is about
          $2,000 less than that of a 2- to 3-year old car.

19. Which of the following expressions could be used to   19.___
    determine how many seconds are in a 24-hour day?
       A. 60 × 60 × 24   B. 60 × 12 × 24
       C. 60 × 2 × 24   D. 60 × 24

20. For measuring milk, we could use each of the following   20.___
    EXCEPT
       A. liters   B. kilograms
       C. millimeters   D. cubic centimeters

21. What is the reading on the gauge   21.___
    shown at the right?
       A. 51
       B. 60
       C. 62.5
       D. 70

22. Bill is taller than Yvonne. Yvonne is shorter than Sue.   22.____
    Sue is 5'4" tall.
    Which of the following conclusions must be TRUE?
       A. Bill is taller than Sue.
       B. Yvonne is taller than 5'4".
       C. Sue is taller than Bill.
       D. Yvonne is the shortest.

23. The Bass family traveled 268 miles during the first day   23.____
    of their vacation and another 300 miles on the next day.
    Maria Bass said they were 568 miles from home.
    Which of the following facts did Maria assume?
       A. They traveled faster on the first day and slower on
          the second.
       B. If she plotted the vacation route on a map, it would
          be a straight line.
       C. Their car used more gasoline on the second day.
       D. They traveled faster on the second day than they did
          on the first day.

24. *The word LEFT in a mathematics problem indicates that it*   24.____
    is a subtraction problem.
    Which of the following mathematics problems proves this
    statement FALSE?
       A. I want to put 150 bottles into cartons which hold
          8 bottles each. After I completely fill as many
          cartons as I can, how many bottles will be left?
       B. Sarah had 5 books but gave one to John. How many
          books did Sarah have left?
       C. Carlos had $4.25 but spent $3.75. How much did he
          have left?
       D. We had 38 models in stock but after yesterday's sale,
          only 12 are left. How many did we sell?

25. Let Q represent the number of miles Dave can jog in 15   25.____
    minutes.
    Identify the expression which represents the number of
    miles Dave can jog between 3:00 PM and 4:45 PM?

    A. $1\frac{3}{4}Q$ B. $7Q$

    C. $15 \times 1\frac{3}{4} \times Q$ D. $\frac{Q}{7}$

___

KEY (CORRECT ANSWERS)

1. C	6. A	11. D	16. B	21. C
2. B	7. C	12. D	17. A	22. D
3. C	8. B	13. C	18. D	23. B
4. C	9. C	14. A	19. A	24. A
5. A	10. B	15. D	20. C	25. B

SOLUTIONS TO PROBLEMS

1. Choice C is in ascending order since .7 < .77 < .777

2. Rewrite in decimal form: .4 + .07 + .005 = .475

3. Let x = missing number. Then, 700x = 7. Solving, $x = \frac{7}{700}$ = .01

4. 943 - 251 = 692 ≈ 700

5. Let x = hours needed. Then, 10/15 = x/6. Solving, x = 4

6. The number of diners (D) is 10 times as many waiters (10W). So, D = 10W or 10W = D

7. Given F = XC + Y, subtract Y from each side to get F - Y = XC. Finally, dividing by X, we get (F-Y)/X = C

8. 12 = 6C/3. Then, 12 = 2C, so C = 6

9. $\frac{5}{7} = \frac{x}{35}$ Then, 7x = 175, so x = 25

10. Probability of a female teacher = $\frac{2}{5}$ = .4

11. Statement D is best, since as time increases, the temperature decreases

12. (3)(2) + 4 = 2Y. Then, 10 = 2Y, so Y = 5

13. Miles per gallon = 243 ÷ 8.7

14. Total purchase is (6)($4) + (4)($5) = $44. The average cost per book is $44 ÷ 10 = $4.40

15. (220)($2.25) = $450. The discount is (.15)($450) = $67.50

16. The number of workdays is 1000 ÷ 125 = 8

17. Choice A is correct because the average duration of the phone calls = total time ÷ total number of calls

18. Statement D is correct since a 4-5 year-old car's value is $4,000, whereas a 2-3 year-old car's value is $6000.

19. 60 seconds = 1 minute and 60 minutes = 1 hour. Thus, 24 hours = (24)(60)(60) or (60)(60)(24) seconds

20. We can't use millimeters in measuring milk since millimeters is a linear measurement

21. The reading shows the average of 50 and 75 = 62.5

22. Since Yvonne is shorter than both Bill and Sue, Yvonne is the shortest.

23. Statement B is assumed correct since 568 = 268 + 300 could only be true if the mileage traveled represents a straight line

24. To find the number of bottles left, we look only for the remainder when 150 is divided by 8 (which happens to be 6)

———

ARITHMETICAL REASONING
EXAMINATION SECTION

DIRECTIONS: Briefly and concisely, solve each of the following problems, using the processes of arithmetic ONLY.

1. It is believed that every even number is the sum of two prime numbers.
   Two prime numbers whose sum is 32 are
   A. 7, 25   B. 11, 21   C. 13, 19   D. 17, 15   1.___

2. To divide a number by 3000, we should move the decimal point 3 places to the _____ by 3.
   A. right and divide   B. left and divide
   C. right and multiply   D. left and multiply   2.___

3. The difference between the area of a rectangle 6 ft. by 4 ft. and the area of a square having the same perimeter is
   A. 1 sq. ft.   B. 2 sq. ft.
   C. 4 sq. ft.   D. none of the above   3.___

4. The ratio of 1/4 to 3/8 is the same as the ratio of
   A. 1 to 3   B. 2 to 3   C. 3 to 2   D. 3 to 4   4.___

5. If $7\frac{1}{2}$ is divided by 1 1/5, the quotient is
   A. $6\frac{1}{4}$ B. 9   C. 7 1/10   D. 6 3/5   5.___

6. A farmer has a cylindrical metal tank for watering his stock. It is 10 ft. in diameter and 3 ft. deep.
   If one cubic foot contains about 7.5 gallons, the APPROXIMATE capacity of the tank, in gallons, is
   A. 12   B. 225   C. 4   D. 1707   6.___

7. The fraction which fits in the following series, 1/2, 1/10, _____, 1/250 is
   A. 1/20   B. 1/100   C. 1/10   D. 1/50   7.___

8. In two years $200 with interest compounded semi-annually at 4% will amount to
   A. $216.48   B. $233.92   C. $208   D. $216   8.___

9. With a tax rate of .0200, a tax bill of $1050 corresponds to an assessed valuation of
   A. $21,000   B. $52,500   C. $21   D. $1029   9.___

10. A sales agent, after deducting his commission of 6%, remits $2491 to his principal.
    The sale amounted to
    A. $2809   B. $2640   C. $2650   D. $2341.54   10.___

11. The percent equivalent of .0295 is
    A. 2.95%   B. 29.5%   C. .295%   D. 295%

11. ___

12. An angle of 105° is a(n) _____ angle.
    A. straight   B. acute   C. obtuse   D. reflex

12. ___

13. A quart is approximately sixty cubic inches. A cubic
    foot of water weighs approximately sixty pounds.
    Therefore, a quart of water weighs APPROXIMATELY _____
    lbs.
    A. 2   B. 3   C. 4   D. 5

13. ___

14. If the same number is added to both the numerator and
    the denominator of a proper fraction, the
    A. value of the fraction is decreased
    B. value of the fraction is increased
    C. value of the fraction is unchanged
    D. effect of the operation depends on the original
       fraction

14. ___

15. The LEAST common multiple of 3, 8, 9, 12 is
    A. 36   B. 72   C. 108   D. 144

15. ___

16. On a bill of $100, the difference between a discount of
    30% and 20% and a discount of 40% and 10% is
    A. nothing   B. $2   C. $20   D. 20%

16. ___

17. 1/3 percent of a number is 24.
    The number is
    A. 8   B. 72   C. 800   D. 7200

17. ___

18. The cost of importing five dozen china dinner sets,
    billed at $32 per set and paying a duty of 40%, is
    A. $224   B. $2688   C. $768   D. $1344

18. ___

19. The net price of a television set is $756.
    If bought with a trade discount of 20%, and 10% for cash,
    the list price is
    A. $925.00   B. $957.80   C. $982.80   D. $1050.00

19. ___

20. If Bob can complete a job in 6 hours and Steven can
    finish it in 8 hours, together they can complete the job
    in _____ hrs. _____ min.
    A. 2; 45   B. 3; 10   C. 3; 25   D. 4; 5

20. ___

21. If the diameter is 80', the APPROXIMATE area of a skating
    rink is _____ square feet.
    A. 251.33   B. 1281.74   C. 2538.77   D. 5026.56

21. ___

22. If an employer is subject to the New York Unemployment
    Insurance Fund and his quarterly payroll totals to $1,800,
    the quarterly tax payable to the Fund would be _____
    (assuming the tax to be 2.7%).
    A. $23.30   B. $48.60   C. $97.70   D. $194.40

22. ___

23. During a certain year, the weekly pay of John Smith was   23.___
    $180, his withholding tax 15%, and his Social Security
    tax was 4.4%.
    Then, Mr. Smith's take-home pay amounted to
        A. $137.17   B. $142.20   C. $145.08   D. $151.13

24. A 5% mortgage of $9,000 is for sale.   24.___
    What will the buyer have to pay for it to net 9%?
        A. $5000   B. $8550   C. $6500   D. $8190

25. If the passenger rate is $54, the operating cost per   25.___
    passenger to the railroad on the basis of 12½% profit
    on fares is
        A. $6.75   B. $38.95   C. $47.25   D. $49.68

26. What is the amount of premium refunded to the insured if   26.___
    the insurance company cancels a 3-year policy at the end
    of 15 months?
    The rate is $30 per year.
        A. $37.50   B. $41.50   C. $43.00   D. $43.75

27. Suits originally selling for $50 were marked down to   27.___
    yield 20% on cost.
    If the original profit was 33 1/3% on cost, the new sales
    price will be
        A. $33.50   B. $40.00   C. $42.75   D. $45.00

28. If he works 10 hours on Tuesday and 12 hours on Friday,   28.___
    and regular hours on the other days, for an 8-hour day,
    5 days per week, daily pay $60, Samuels will earn
    _____ (time and a half for overtime).
        A. $ 300   B. $ 367.50   C. $ 375   D. $ 392.50

29. To provide 10,000 typewriting sheets (8½ x 11), the mill   29.___
    will have to cut how many reams of folio stock which
    measures 17 x 22?
        A. 5   B. 6½   C. 8   D. 10

30. Property worth $16,000 was insured for $10,000 under a   30.___
    policy containing the 80% co-insurance clause. The
    damage amounted to $9,600.
    The insured will collect
        A. $4800   B. $6500   C. $7500   D. $7800

31. At the rate of $1.68 for the Sterling, what will the   31.___
    traveler require in American currency to meet expenses
    and purchases of goods calling for £20 6s. 6d?
        A. $21.34   B. $34.15   C. $38.21   D. $57.12

32. The proceeds of a 6% interest-bearing note for $800 due   32.___
    in 45 days and discounted 15 days after it was dated, at
    the rate of 5%, will be
        A. $796.25   B. $802.64   C. $804.93   D. $805.92

33. $4.80 is .08% of
    A. $600   B. $6000   C. $6500   D. $60,000

33.___

34. If 25% of a classroom register consists of boys, the ratio of girls to boys is
    A. 4:1   B. 3:1   C. 1:4   D. 1:3

34.___

35. If a wage earner who is over 65 years of age, married (wife's age 55) and 2 other dependents whose earnings are below $2,300, pays his Federal income tax, what will his TOTAL exemptions add up to?
    A. 2   B. 3   C. 4   D. 5

35.___

36. An equality of ratios is another term for
    A. proportion   B. equilibrium
    C. summation   D. inversion

36.___

37. A kilometer is APPROXIMATELY what part of a mile?
    A. 0.059   B. 0.062   C. 0.064   D. 0.067

37.___

38. Two liters is a _____ quantity than two quarts.
    A. smaller dry quart/larger liquid quart
    B. larger dry quart/smaller liquid quart
    C. smaller dry quart/smaller liquid quart
    D. larger dry quart/larger liquid quart

38.___

39. The square root of 46.24 is
    A. 6.793   B. 6.800   C. 7.984   D. 9.248

39.___

40. Ordinary interest is _____ than exact interest for the same time and at the same rate.
    A. less   B. more   C. equal   D. variable

40.___

41. After all taxes have been added on, what will the coat cost the purchaser if the advertised price of a natural mink coat is $8,000? (Assume Federal Sales Tax is 10% and the Local Sales Tax is 8¼%.)
    A. $8660   B. $9460   C. $9526   D. $9548

41.___

42. A ring bearing the mark 12K on the inside contains _____ parts gold and 12 parts alloy.
    A. 2   B. 12   C. 6   D. 14

42.___

43. The sounding line recorded a depth of 20 fathoms or _____ feet.
    A. 110   B. 120   C. 130   D. 140

43.___

44. If a pound of green peanuts costs $1.25 and peanuts lose 1/6 of its weight in the roasting process, what is the cost of the roasted peanuts?
    A. $1.00   B. $1.20   C. $1.25   D. $1.50

44.___

45. A cubic foot (liquid measure) is APPROXIMATELY how many   45. ___
    gallons?
         A. 7.48   B. 7.55   C. 7.65   D. 7.80

46. If the closing price of USX Corp. reads 76½ followed by   46. ___
    -¼, it indicates that the previous day's closing price was
         A. 76 3/4   B. 76½   C. 76 5/8   D. 76 3/8

47. An inscription on the cornerstone of a building reads   ·   47. ___
    MDCXCIV.
    This means that the cornerstone was placed there in the
    year
         A. 1484   B. 1594   C. 1694   D. 1794

48. 12 plus 6 × 6 less 24 ÷ 6 plus 10 equals   48. ___
         A. 44   B. 64   C. 54   D. 14

49. A motorist travels 120 miles to his destination at the   49. ___
    average speed of 60 miles per hour and returns to the
    starting point at the average speed of 40 miles per hour.
    His AVERAGE speed for the entire trip is _____ miles per
    hour.
         A. 53   B. 50   C. 48   D. 45

50. A snapshot measures 2½ inches by 1 7/8 inches. It is to   50. ___
    be enlarged so that the longer dimension will be 4 inches.
    The length of the enlarged shorter dimension will be
    _____ inches.
         A. 2½   B. 3 3/8
         C. 3   D. none of the above

KEY (CORRECT ANSWERS)

1. C	11. A	21. D	31. B	41. B
2. B	12. C	22. D	32. B	42. B
3. A	13. A	23. C	33. B	43. B
4. B	14. B	24. A	34. B	44. D
5. A	15. B	25. C	35. C	45. A
6. B	16. B	26. D	36. A	46. A
7. D	17. D	27. D	37. B	47. C
8. A	18. B	28. B	38. A	48. C
9. B	19. D	29. A	39. B	49. C
10. C	20. C	30. C	40. B	50. C

SOLUTIONS TO PROBLEMS

1. CORRECT ANSWER: C
    A prime number is an integer which cannot be divided except
    by itself and one integer; a whole number as opposed to a
    fraction or a decimal.

2. CORRECT ANSWER: B

    $$\begin{array}{r} 2 \\ \hline 3)\overline{6.000}. \end{array}$$ Example: Divide 6000 by 3000

3. CORRECT ANSWER: A

     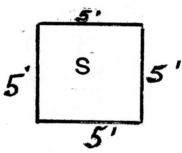

    P = 20 ft.   P = 20 ft.
    A = 24 sq. ft.   A = 25 sq. ft.

    $$\begin{array}{r} 25 \\ -24 \\ \hline 1 \end{array}$$

4. CORRECT ANSWER: B

    $$\dfrac{1/4}{3/8} = 1/4 \div 3/8 = 1/4 \times 8/3 = 2/3$$

5. CORRECT ANSWER: A

    $$\dfrac{7\frac{1}{2}}{1\ 1/5} = \dfrac{15}{2} \div \dfrac{6}{5} = \dfrac{15}{2} \times \dfrac{5}{6} = \dfrac{25}{4} = 6\frac{1}{4}$$

                          OR

    $$\begin{array}{r} 6\ \frac{3}{12}\ \frac{1}{4} \\ \hline 1.2)\overline{7.5} \end{array}$$

6. CORRECT ANSWER: B

    A = πR^2 $\pi = \dfrac{22}{7} = 3$ (approx.)
      = $3(5)^2$
      = 75 sq. ft.   Volume of tank = 75 × 3 =
                             225 cu. ft.
    $$\begin{array}{r} 225 \\ \times 7.5 \\ \hline 1125 \\ 1575 \\ \hline 1687.5 \text{ gal.} \end{array}$$ (approximate capacity of
                         tank in gallons)

7. CORRECT ANSWER: D
A geometric series: each number is multiplied by the same
number to get the succeeding number.
(Multiply each number by 1/5.)

1/2, 1/10, 1/50, 1/250

8. CORRECT ANSWER: A
Compound Interest
4% a year compounded semi-annually is the same as 2% for a
half year.

(a) $200
    ×.02
    $4.00 Interest for 1st half year

$200
+ 4
$204 Principal for 1st half yea

(b) $204
    ×.02
    $4.08 Interest for 2nd half year

$204.00
+ 4.08
$208.08 Principal for 1st half
        of 2nd year

(c) $208.08
    ×   .02
    $4.1616 Interest for 1st half
            of 2nd year

$208.08
+ 4.16
$212.24 Principal for 2nd
        half of 2nd year

(d) $212.24
    ×   .02
    $4.2448 Interest for 2nd half
            of 2nd year

$212.24
+ 4.24
$216.48 Principal at end of
        2nd half of 2nd year

9. CORRECT ANSWER: B
.0200x = $1050
 200x = $10,500,000
   2x = $105,000
    x = $52,500 (assessed valuation)

10. CORRECT ANSWER: C
$2491 + .06x = x
x = 2491 + .06x
1.00x - .06x = 2491
.94x = 2491
 94x = 249,100

       $2,650
94)249,100

Proof
$2650
× .06
$159.00

$2491
+ 159
$2650

11. CORRECT ANSWER: A
.0295 = 2.95%

12. CORRECT ANSWER: C
An obtuse angle is an angle greater than 90°.

13. CORRECT ANSWER: A

A quart = 60 cu. in.
80 lbs. = 1 cu. ft. (or 1728 cu.in.)(12×12×12)
          (Keep like units of measure together)
60 lbs. = 1728 cu.in.
1 lb.   = $\frac{1728}{60}$ = approximately .29 cu. in.

If 29 cu.in. weigh 1 lb., then 60 cu.in. weighs 2 lbs. (approx).
Therefore, a quart weighs 2 lbs. (approx.).

14. CORRECT ANSWER: B

(1) Start with the fraction 2/3

(2) $\frac{2 + 2}{3 + 2} = \frac{4}{5}$ (Adding 2 to the numerator and the denominator)

(3) $\frac{2}{3} = \frac{10}{15}$

(4) $\frac{4}{5} = \frac{12}{15}$

15. CORRECT ANSWER: B

Common multiple: can be evenly divided by all the numbers.
Least common multiple: the lowest of these numbers (72).

16. CORRECT ANSWER: B

Formula

    Step 1. Express percentages as decimals
    Step 2. Subtract each discount from one
    Step 3. Multiply all the results
    Step 4. Subtract the product from one

    Step 1. .3, .2, and .4, .1
    Step 2. .7, .8, and .6, .9
    Step 3. .7 × .8 = .56 (represents percent remaining after the
            .6 × .9 = .54 discounts are taken)
    Step 4. 1.00   1.00
            −.56   −.54
             .44   .46
      The difference is 2%
Then, $100 × .02 = $2.00.

17. CORRECT ANSWER: D

$\frac{1}{300}x = 24$

x = 24 × 300

x = 7200

18. CORRECT ANSWER: B

$32
× 60
$1920   (Cost of dinner sets before paying duty)

$1920
× .40
$768.00 (Duty)

$1920
+ 768
$2688

19. CORRECT ANSWER: D
Single discount for 20% and 10% = 28%
20 + 10 = 30
20 × 10% = 2.0
28.0

List Price - Discount = Net Price
100% - 28% = 72%
$756 = 72% of List Price

```
        1050
72)$75600
    72
     360
     360
```

20. CORRECT ANSWER: C

$\frac{1}{6} + \frac{1}{8} = \frac{7}{24}$ (job done in 1 hour by both)

∴ $24 ÷ 7 = 3\frac{3}{7}$ (hours together)

= 3 hours, 25 minutes

21. CORRECT ANSWER: D
Area = Πr^2
= $3.1416 × (40')^2$ = 3.1416 × 1600 = 5026.56 sq. ft.

22. CORRECT ANSWER: B
1800 × 2.7% = $48.60 (quarterly) or $194.40 (annually)

23. CORRECT ANSWER: C
(1) $180 × 15% = $27.00 (Withholding Tax)
(2) $180 × 4.4% = $ 7.92 (Social Security Tax)
                  $34.92 (Total Tax Deduction)

$180 - $34.92 = $145.08 (Take-home Pay)

24. CORRECT ANSWER: A
5% of $9,000 = $450 (income for 1 year)
To obtain 9%, the cost of the mortgage must be:

$$450 = \frac{9}{100} \text{ of the mortgage}$$

$$450 \times \frac{100}{9} = \$5000 \text{ (cost of mortgage)}$$

25. CORRECT ANSWER: C
Passenger rate = $54
Profit   =   6.75 (1/8 of 54)
Operating Cost = $47.25

26. CORRECT ANSWER: D
30 × 2½ = $75 (premium for 3 years)
36 months – 15 months = 21 months unexpired time

$$\frac{21}{36} \times 75 = \$43.75 \text{ (amount to be refunded)}$$

27. CORRECT ANSWER: D
L.P.   = $50 = 133 1/3% of cost
Cost   = 100%
Profit = 33 1/3%

          50 = 1 1/3 of the cost
      50 × 3/4 = $37.50 cost
   $37.50 × 1/5 = $7.50 new profit
$37.50 + $7.50 = $45.00 new marked price

28. CORRECT ANSWER: B

	Regular Time	Overtime
Monday	8	
Tuesday	8	2
Wednesday	8	
Thursday	8	
Friday	8	4
	40 hours	6 hours

Rate per hour = $60 / 8 hours = $7.50 per hour
Overtime = 6 hours × 1½ × $7.50 =$11.25 overtime pay x 6 hrs.=$67
Payment for regular time worked = 40 hours × $7.50 = $300.00
Samuels earned $67.50 + $300 = $ 367.50

29. CORRECT ANSWER: A
500 sheets   = 1 ream of paper
1 ream 17×22   = 4 sheets 8½×11
500 sheets × 4 = 2000 sheets from 1 ream (17×22)
∴ 10,000 sheets may be obtained from 5 reams (17×22)

30. CORRECT ANSWER: C

$$\frac{10,000}{4/5 \times 16,000} \times 9,600 = \$7,500$$

31. CORRECT ANSWER: B   (12 pence (d) = 1 shilling(s);
    6s = .3£   20 s = 1 pound (£);
    .5s = .025£   6d = .5s)
          .325£

    ∴ $1.68 × 20.325£ = $34.15

32. CORRECT ANSWER: B
    Maturation value of $800 note at 6% interest for 45 days may
    be computed as follows:
      $800 + (1/8 × .06 × 800) = 800 + 6 = $806 (maturation value)

    Interest is $8.06 for 72 days at 5%
    Interest is $4.03 for 36 days at 5%
    Interest is   .67 for 6 days at 5%
    Interest is $3.36 for 30 days at 5%

    Finally, maturation value = $806.00
                    discount =   3.36
                    proceeds = $802.64

33. CORRECT ANSWER: B
    $4.80 ÷ .0008 = $6000

34. CORRECT ANSWER: B
    Boys = 1/4 of class
    ∴ Girls = 3/4 of class
    Ratio is 3 to 1 (girls to boys)

35. CORRECT ANSWER: C
    Exemptions: 1 + 1 + 2 = 4

36. CORRECT ANSWER: A
    Proportion

37. CORRECT ANSWER: B
    39.37 inches = 1 meter
    3937 inches = 1 kilometer
    1 kilometer = 3937 ÷ 12 = 328.08 ft.
    ∴ 328.08 ÷ 5280 = .0621

38. CORRECT ANSWER: A
    1 liter = 0.9081 U.S. dry quart   ANSWER: Smaller (U.S. dry quart)
    1 liter = 1.0567 U.S. liquid quarts ANSWER: Larger (U.S. liquid
                                                          quart)

39. CORRECT ANSWER: B
          6.8
    22)46.24

         36
    128)1024
        1024

40. CORRECT ANSWER: B
More

41. CORRECT ANSWER: B
$8000 + $800 (Federal Tax 10%) + $660 (Local Sales Tax 3%) = $946

42. CORRECT ANSWER: B
Gold marked 12K is 12/24 pure and 12/24 alloy.

43. CORRECT ANSWER: B
1 fathom = 6 feet

44. CORRECT ANSWER: D
Cost = $1.25, which is 5/6 of the cost of the roasted peanuts
$\therefore$ $1.25 × 6/5 = $1.50, the cost of 1 lb. of roasted peanuts.

45. CORRECT ANSWER: A
231 cu.in. = 1 gallon
1 cu.ft. = 12"×12"×12" = 1728 cu.in.
1728 ÷ 231 = 7.48 gallons

46. CORRECT ANSWER: A
$76\frac{1}{2} + \frac{1}{4}$ = 76 3/4 (previous day's closing)

47. CORRECT ANSWER: C
M = 1000
DC = 600
XC =   90
IV =   4
      ____
      1694

48. CORRECT ANSWER: C
12 + 36 - 4 + 10 = 54

Order of Operations:
In order to find the value of a number expression:
 1. First, do all the multiplications
 2. Second, do the divisions, taking them in order from left
    to right
 3. Finally, do the additions and subtractions, taking them
    in any order

49. CORRECT ANSWER: C
120 miles = 2 hours (60 mph)
120 miles = 3 hours (40 mph)
240 miles = 5 hours = average of 48 mph

50. CORRECT ANSWER: C
Change $2\frac{1}{2}$ to $\frac{20}{8}$

Change 1 7/8 to $\frac{15}{8}$

Ratio is 20 to 15 or 4 to 3

If the longer dimension is 4 inches, then the shorter is 3 inches

EXAMINATION SECTION

DIRECTIONS: Each question or incomplete statement is followed by several suggested answers or completions. Select the one that BEST answers the question or completes the statement. *PRINT THE LETTER OF THE CORRECT ANSWER IN THE SPACE AT THE RIGHT.*

1. To check the correctness of the answer to a multiplication example, divide the
    A. product by the multiplier
    B. multiplier by the product
    C. multiplicand by the multiplier
    D. multiplier by the multiplicand

1.___

2. Of the following correct ways to solve .125 × .32, the MOST efficient is to
    A. write .125 under .32, multiply, point off 5 places
    B. write .32 under .125, multiply, point off 5 places
    C. multiply 125 by 32 and divide by 1000 × 100
    D. divide .32 by 8

2.___

3. If you were to eat each meal in a different restaurant in the city's eating places, assuming that you eat three meals a day, it would take you more than 19 years to cover all of the city's eating places.
On the basis of this information, the BEST of the following choices is that the number of restaurants in the city
    A. exceeds 20,500
    B. is closer to 21,000 than 22,000
    C. exceeds 21,000
    D. does not exceed 21,500

3.___

4. The cost of electricity for operating an 875 watt toaster, an 1100 watt steam iron, and four 75 watt lamps, each for one hour, at 7.5 cents per kilowatt hour (1 kilowatt equals 1000 watts) is
    A. 15¢   B. 17¢   C. $1.54   D. $1.71

4.___

5. Of the following, the pair that is NOT a set of equivalents is
    A. .021%, .00021   B. ¼%, .0025
    C. 1.5%, 3/200   D. 225%, .225

5.___

6. Assuming that the series will continue in the same pattern, the NEXT number in the series 3, 5, 11, 29, ... is
    A. 41   B. 47   C. 65   D. 83

6.___

7. If the total area of a picture measuring 10 inches by 12 inches plus a matting of uniform width surrounding the picture is 224 square inches, the width of the matting is ____ inches.
    A. 2   B. 2 4/11   C. 3   D. 4

7.___

8. The net price of a $25 item after successive discounts   8. ___
of 20% and 30% is
   A. $11   B. $12.50   C. $14   D. $19

9. The cost of 63 inches of ribbon at 12¢ per yard is   9. ___
   A. $.20   B. $.21   C. $.22   D. $.23

10. If $1\frac{1}{2}$ cups of cereal are used with $4\frac{1}{2}$ cups of water, the   10. ___
amount of water needed with 3/4 of a cup of cereal is
____ cups.
   A. 2   B. 2 1/8   C. $2\frac{1}{4}$ D. $2\frac{1}{2}$

11. Under certain conditions, sound travels at about 1100 ft.   11. ___
per second.
If 88 ft. per second is approximately equivalent to 60
miles per hour, the speed of sound, under the above
conditions, is, of the following, CLOSEST to ____ miles
per hour.
   A. 730   B. 740   C. 750   D. 760

12. Of the following, the MOST NEARLY accurate set of   12. ___
equivalents is
   A. 1 foot equals 30.48 centimeters
   B. 1 centimeter equals 2.54 inches
   C. 1 rod equals 3.28 meters
   D. 1 meter equals 1.09 feet

13. If one angle of a triangle is three times a second angle   13. ___
and the third angle is 20° more than the second angle,
the second angle is
   A. 32°   B. 34°   C. 40°   D. 50°

14. Assuming that on a blueprint $\frac{1}{4}$ inch equals 12 inches, the   14. ___
ACTUAL length, in feet, of a steel bar represented on the
blueprint by a line 3 3/8 inches long is
   A. 3 3/8   B. 6 3/4   C. $12\frac{1}{2}$ D. $13\frac{1}{2}$

15. A plane leaves Denver, Colorado on June 1st at 1 P.M.   15. ___
Mountain Standard Time and arrives at New York City on
June 2nd at 2 A.M. Eastern Daylight Savings Time.
The ACTUAL time of flight was ____ hours.
   A. 10   B. 11   C. 12   D. 13

16. Of the following, the CLOSEST to that of $\frac{42.10 \times .0003}{.002}$ 16. ___
is
   A. .063   B. .63   C. 6.3   D. 63

17. If Mrs. Jones bought 3 3/4 yards of dacron at $1.16 per   17. ___
yard and 4 2/3 yards of velvet at $3.87 per yard, the
amount of change she receives from $25 is
   A. $2.12   B. $2.28   C. $2.59   D. $2.63

18. The water level of a swimming pool 75 feet by 42 feet is   18.____
to be raised 4 inches.
The number of gallons of water needed for this purpose is
(1 cubic foot equals 7½ gallons)
    A. 140   B. 7,875   C. 31,500   D. 94,500

19. The part of the total quantity represented by a 24 degree   19.____
sector of a circle graph is
    A. 6 2/3%   B. 12%   C. 13 1/3%   D. 24%

20. If the shipping charges to a certain point are 62 cents   20.____
for the first 5 oz. and 8 cents for each additional ounce,
the weight of a package for which the charges are $1.66 is
    A. 13 oz.   B. 1 1/8 lbs.   C. 1¼ lbs.   D. 1½ lbs.

21. If 15 cans of food are needed for 7 men for 2 days, the   21.____
number of cans needed for 4 men for 7 days is
    A. 15   B. 20   C. 25   D. 30

22. The total saving in purchasing thirty 13¢ ice cream pops   22.____
for a class party at a reduced rate of $1.38 per dozen is
    A. 35¢   B. 40¢   C. 45¢   D. 50¢

23. The quotient for the division of 36 apples among 4 children   23.____
may be CORRECTLY found by thinking ____
    A. $36 \div \frac{1}{4}$ B. $36\overline{)4.0}$
    C. $\frac{1}{4}$ of 36   D. 4/36

24. The missing term in the equation 1/3 of ? = ½ of 90 is   24.____
    A. 45   B. 30   C. 15   D. 135

25. The fraction CLOSEST to 4/5 is   25.____
    A. 2/3   B. 7/9   C. 8/11   D. 5/8

26. Of the following, the one which may be used CORRECTLY to   26.____
compute the value of 4 × 22½ is
    A. (4 × 45) + (4 × ½)
    B. (4 × ½) + (4 × 2) + (4 × 2)
    C. (½ of 4) + (2 × 4) + (2 × 4)
    D. (4 × 20) + (4 × 2) + (4 × ½)

27. 16½ ÷ ¼ may CORRECTLY be expressed as   27.____
    A. (¼ × 16) + (¼ × ½)   B. (4 × 16) + (4 × ½)
    C. $4\overline{)16.5}$ D. ¼ times 33/2

28. In computation, 3/4 may be CORRECTLY transformed into   28.____
6/8 for the same reason that
    A. 7(3+4) = 21 + 28   B. 3 apples + 5 apples = 8
    C. $.2\overline{)3.4} = 2\overline{)34}$ D. 3 + 4 = 4 + 3

29. The mathematical law of distribution is illustrated by   29.____
all of the following EXCEPT

A. 15	B. 15	C. 15	D. 15
×12	×12	×12	×12
150	30	180	30
30	150		15
180	180		180

30. Of the following series of partial sums which might arise in the addition of 36 and 25, the one that is INCORRECT is
    A. 11, 31, 61　　　　　　B. 11, 4, 6, 61
    C. 11, 41, 61　　　　　　D. 36, 56, 61

30.___

31. Of the following, the one which equals one million is
    A. ten hundred thousand
    B. 10^7
    C. $10 \times 10 \times 10 \times 10 \times 10 \times 10 \times 10$
    D. 1 plus 6 zeroes

31.___

32. Of the following groups, the one containing four terms all associated with one algorismic process is
    A. addend, quotient, dividend, divisor
    B. dividend, quotient, divisor, minuend
    C. dividend, quotient, addend, minuend
    D. multiplicand, product, minuend, addend

32.___

33. Depreciation of a certain machine is estimated, for any year, at 20% of its value at the beginning of the year. If the machine is purchased for $600, its estimated net value at the end of two years is CLOSEST to
    A. $325　　　B. $350　　　C. $375　　　D. $400

33.___

34. Hats are purchased at the rate of $33 per dozen. If they are sold at a close-out sale for $2.50 each, the percent loss on the cost price is
    A. 3　　　B. 3 1/3　　　C. 9 1/11　　　D. 10

34.___

35. The time 3 hours, 58 minutes after 10:56 A.M. is ____ P.M.
    A. 4:54　　　B. 2:54　　　C. 4:14　　　D. 2:14

35.___

36. Mr. Brown had $20.00 when he took his three children on a bus trip. He spent $7.33 for the four tickets and bought each of the children a magazine costing 15¢, a candy bar costing 11¢, and a 5¢ package of chewing gum. His change from the $20.00 was
    A. $12.74　　　B. $11.43　　　C. $11.74　　　D. $12.84

36.___

37. The loan value on a life insurance policy at the end of five years is $30.19 per $1000 of insurance. The LARGEST amount, to the nearest dollar, that can be borrowed on a $5500 policy at the end of five years is
    A. $17　　　B. $151　　　C. $166　　　D. $1660

37.___

38. Using cups that hold six ounces of milk, the number of cupfuls a person can obtain from $1\frac{1}{2}$ gallons of milk is
    A. 16　　　B. 24　　　C. 32　　　D. 64

38.___

39. A storekeeper purchased an article for $36. In order to include 10% of cost for overhead and to provide $9 of net profit, the markup should be
    A. 25%　　　B. 35%　　　C. $37\frac{1}{2}$%　　　D. 40%

39.___

40. A rectangular carton has twice the height, one-third the length, and four times the width of a second carton. The ratio of the volume of the first carton to that of the second carton is 40.___
    A. 16:3   B. 2:1   C. 8:3   D. 3:8

41. If $300 is invested at simple interest so as to yield interest income of $18 in 9 months, the amount of money that must be invested at the same rate of interest so as to yield a return of $120 in 6 months is 41.___
    A. $3000   B. $3300   C. $2800   D. $2400

42. If a boy has a number of dimes and quarters in his pocket adding up to $3.10, the LARGEST possible number of dimes he can have is 42.___
    A. 16   B. 28   C. 26   D. 21

43. In a number system using the base 10, the value represented by the first digit 3 reading from the left in the number 82,364,371 is ____ times the value represented by the second digit 3. 43.___
    A. 30   B. 100   C. 1,000   D. 10,000

44. The number of revolutions made by a bicycle wheel of 28 inch diameter in traveling $\frac{1}{2}$ mile is CLOSEST to 44.___
    A. 720   B. 180   C. 360   D. 120

45. Of the following, the property which is TRUE of all parallelograms is that the 45.___
    A. diagonals are equal
    B. diagonals meet at right angles
    C. sum of the interior angles is 180°
    D. diagonals bisect each other

46. Of the following explanations about steps in the computation at the right, the one which is LEAST meaningful or accurate is that the 46.___

$$\begin{array}{r} 218 \\ 32\overline{)6985} \\ 64 \\ \hline 58 \\ 32 \\ \hline 265 \\ 256 \\ \hline 9 \end{array}$$

    A. 64 represents 200 × 32
    B. 265 is the result of subtracting 320 from 585
    C. 9 is part of the quotient
    D. 256 symbolizes the subtraction of 32 eight times

47. Assuming that a system of meridians and parallels of latitude like that used on maps of the earth's surface was designed for the moon's surface, the distance covered by a man traveling 1° on the moon as compared to that covered in traveling 1° on the earth would be 47.___
    A. equal
    B. less
    C. greater
    D. sometimes greater and sometimes less

48. 1958 may MOST correctly be expressed in Roman numerals as   48.___
    A. MDCDLVIII   B. CMMLVIII   C. MCMLVIII   D. MCMLIIX

49. If the same positive quantity is added to both the   49.___
numerator and the denominator of a proper fraction, the
value of the new fraction, as compared to that of the
original fraction, will be
    A. greater   B. less
    C. equal   D. either greater or less

50. If the Fahrenheit temperature is 74°, the Centigrade   50.___
equivalent would be [Use the formula $C = 5/9 (F-32)$]
    A. 9 1/9°   B. 23 1/3°   C. 42°   D. 56 2/9°

KEY (CORRECT ANSWERS)

1. A	11. C	21. D	31. A	41. A
2. D	12. A	22. C	32. B	42. C
3. A	13. A	23. C	33. C	43. C
4. B	14. D	24. D	34. C	44. C
5. D	15. A	25. B	35. B	45. D
6. D	16. C	26. D	36. C	46. C
7. C	17. C	27. B	37. C	47. B
8. A	18. B	28. C	38. C	48. C
9. B	19. A	29. C	39. B	49. A
10. C	20. B	30. B	40. C	50. B

SOLUTIONS TO PROBLEMS

1. CORRECT ANSWER: A
```
     12 (multiplicand)
   ×  2 (multiplier)
     24 (product)
```

2. CORRECT ANSWER: D
The most efficient way is to divide .32 by 8.
.125 = .12½ = 12½% = 1/8
$$1/8 X \quad .32 = \frac{.32}{8} = 8\overline{)\,.32}^{\,.04}$$
```
                          .32
```

3. CORRECT ANSWER: A
```
     365 (days in 1 year)            4 (leap-year days)
   ×   3 (meals)                    × 3 (meals)
    1095 (meals in 1 year)          12 (leap-year meals)
   ×  19 (number of years)
  20,805 (number of meals eaten in 19 years)
   +  12 (number of meals eaten in leap years)
  20,817 (total)
```

4. CORRECT ANSWER: B
```
     875 watts
    1100
     300
    2275 ÷ 1000 = 2 11/40 kw. hours
```

2 11/40 × 7.5 = .17 (approximately)

5. CORRECT ANSWER: D
A. .021% = .00021
B. ¼% = 1/400 = $400\overline{)1.0000}^{\,.0025}$
C. 1.5% = .015 = $\dfrac{15}{1000} = \dfrac{3}{200}$
D. 225% = 2.25, NOT .225

6. CORRECT ANSWER: D
Suggestions for Series Problems
1. Find the difference between the numbers (or squares of differences).
2. In this series, each difference is multiplied by 3 and added to the succeeding number.

```
     3,5  The difference is 2
            3 × 2 = 6
            5 + 6 = 11
```

5, 11   The difference is 6
          3 × 6 = 18
          11 + 18 = 29

11, 29   The difference is 18
          3 × 18 = 54
          29 + 54 = 83

7. CORRECT ANSWER: C
Total area = 224 square inches

```
    16"
  ×  14"
    64
    16
   224  square inches
```

8. CORRECT ANSWER: A
Solution

Successive discounts
  20%, 30%

1. Convert to decimals .2, .3
2. Subtract from 1.0   .8, .7
3. Multiply .8 × .7 = .56
4. 1.00 - .56 = .44

```
   25.00
  ×  .44
     100
   100
  $11.00
```

∴ $25 - $11 = $14

Alternate Solution

```
    $25
  × .20
  $5.00
```

$25 - 5 = $20.00

```
    $20
  × .30
  $6.00
```

$20 - $6 = $14 ANSWER

9. CORRECT ANSWER: B

$63" = \dfrac{63}{36}$ yards

$\begin{matrix} 21 \\ \cancel{63} \\ \cancel{36} \\ 3 \end{matrix} \times \begin{matrix} .01 \\ .\cancel{12} \end{matrix} = 21¢$

Alternate Solution

12¢ per yard

$\dfrac{12}{36} = \dfrac{1}{3}¢$ per inch

$\dfrac{63"}{1} \times \dfrac{1}{3}¢ = \dfrac{63}{3} = 21¢$

10. CORRECT ANSWER: C

Proportion

	Cereal	Water
1st mixture	1½ cups	4½ cups
2nd mixture	3/4 cups	x cups

3/4 is half of 1½
Therefore, half of 4½ is 2¼

11. CORRECT ANSWER: C
The speed of sound is 1100 ft. per second.
88 ft. per second = 60 miles an hour

$\frac{1100}{88}$ = indicates the number of times greater than 60 miles an
hour is the speed of sound

$$\begin{array}{r} 12\frac{1}{2} \text{ times} \\ 88\overline{)1100} \end{array}$$

$$\begin{array}{r} 60 \\ \times\ 12\frac{1}{2} \\ \hline 750 \text{ miles per hour} \end{array}$$

12. CORRECT ANSWER: A
Conversion
A meter = 39 inches (39.37 inches)
     = 3¼ ft. ($\frac{39}{12}$ = 3¼)

A centimeter = .39 inches

1 rod = 5½ yards   (5.5 yards × 3 = 16.5 feet)
     = 16½ feet

A rod is approximately 5 meters (See choice (C) which is,
                                     therefore, wrong)

A meter is 100 centimeters (one cm. = .01)
3¼ feet = 1 meter or 100 centimeters

$1 \text{ ft} = \frac{100}{3\frac{1}{4}} = \frac{100}{1} + \frac{13}{4} = \frac{100}{1} \times \frac{4}{13} = \frac{400}{13}$

$$\begin{array}{r} 30.76 \\ 13\overline{)400.00} \end{array}$$

13. CORRECT ANSWER: A
Let x = 2nd angle
Let 3x = 1st angle
Let x + 20° = 3rd angle

$$3x + x + x + 20 = 180$$
$$5x + 20 = 180$$
$$5x = 160$$
$$x = 32°$$

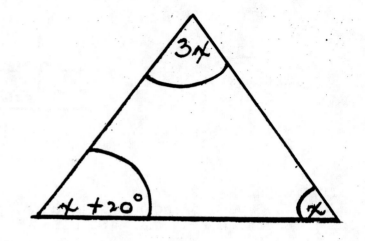

14. CORRECT ANSWER: D

$$\frac{\frac{1}{4}''}{12} = \frac{3\ 3/8''}{x}$$

$\frac{1}{4} \div 12/1 = 27/8 \div x/1$

$\frac{1}{4} \times 1/12 = 27/8 \times 1/x$

$\frac{1}{4} = 27/8x$
$8x = 48 \times 27 = 1296$
$x = 162$ inches
$= 13\frac{1}{2}$ ft.

15. CORRECT ANSWER: A

Time Belts

PACIFIC	MOUNTAIN	CENTRAL	EASTERN
4 A.M.	5 A.M.	6 A.M.	7 A.M. E.S.T.
			8 A.M. D.S.T.

In traveling eastward, we set our clocks forward for each time zone.

Plane left at 1 P.M.
Traveled around clock 12 hours or 13 hours at 2 A.M.
Subtract 2 hours difference between Mountain Time and Eastern Standard Time. Subtract another hour for Daylight Savings Time. That is, 13 - 3 = 10 hours.

16. CORRECT ANSWER: C

$$\frac{42.10 \times .0003}{.002} = \frac{42 \times .0003}{.002} \quad \text{(approximating)}$$

Work

$$\begin{array}{r} 42 \\ \times\, .0003 \\ \hline .0126 \end{array} = \frac{.0126}{.002} = \frac{12.6}{2} = 6.3$$

17. CORRECT ANSWER: C

$$\begin{array}{r} \$1.16 \\ \times\ \ 3\ 3/4 \\ \hline \$4.35 \end{array} \qquad \begin{array}{r} \$3.87 \\ \times\ \ 4\ 2/3 \\ \hline \$18.06 \end{array} \qquad \begin{array}{r} \$18.06 \\ +\ 4.35 \\ \hline \$22.41 \end{array} \qquad \begin{array}{r} \$25.00 \\ -22.41 \\ \hline \$\ 2.59 \end{array}$$

18. CORRECT ANSWER: B

$42 \times 75 \times 1/3$ ft (4") = 1050 cu.ft.

$$\begin{array}{r} \times\ \ 7\frac{1}{2} \\ \hline 7875 \text{ gallons} \end{array}$$

19. CORRECT ANSWER: A

$$\frac{24}{360} = \frac{2}{30} = \frac{1}{15} = .06\ 2/3 = 6\ 2/3\%$$

20. CORRECT ANSWER: B

$$\begin{array}{l} \$1.66 \text{ total charge} \\ -\ .62 \text{ 1st 5 oz.} \\ \hline \$1.04 \text{ charge at 8 cents an oz.} \end{array} \qquad \qquad .08)\overline{\$1.04}\ \ ^{13\text{ oz.}}$$

$$\begin{array}{r} 13 \text{ oz} \\ +\ 5 \text{ oz} \\ \hline 18 \text{ oz.} \end{array} \qquad \frac{18}{16} = 1\ \frac{2}{16} = \frac{1}{8} \text{ lb.}$$

21. CORRECT ANSWER: D

Cans	Men	Days	Number of days one man would need to consume the cans
15	7	2	14 days
x	4	7	28 days

x = 2(15) = 30 cans

22. CORRECT ANSWER: C

$$
\begin{array}{r}
\$\ .13 \\
\times\ \ 30 \\
\hline
\$3.90 \\
-3.45 \\
\hline
\$\ .45
\end{array}
$$

$\dfrac{30}{12} = 2\frac{1}{2}$ dozens

$$
\begin{array}{r}
\$1.38 \\
\times\ \ \ 2\frac{1}{2} \\
\hline
\$3.45
\end{array}
$$

23. CORRECT ANSWER: C

$\dfrac{36}{4} = 9$

24. CORRECT ANSWER: D

1/3 of ? = $\frac{1}{2}$ of 90

$$
\begin{aligned}
1/3x &= 45 \\
x &= 3 \times 45 \\
&= 135
\end{aligned}
$$

25. CORRECT ANSWER: B

$$
\begin{aligned}
4/5 &= .80 \\
2/3 &= .66 \\
7/9 &= .78 \\
8/11 &= .73 \\
5/8 &= .63
\end{aligned}
$$

26. CORRECT ANSWER: D

$$
\begin{array}{r}
22\frac{1}{2} \\
\times\ 4 \\
\hline
80 \\
8 \\
2 \\
\hline
90
\end{array}
$$

Choice (D) $(4 \times 20) + (4 \times 2) + (4 \times \frac{1}{2}) = 80 + 8 + 2 = 90$
(This is an example of the Distributive Law, which links
the operations of addition and multiplication.)

27. CORRECT ANSWER: B

$16\frac{1}{2} \div 4 = \dfrac{16\frac{1}{2}}{4} = 16\frac{1}{2} \times 4/1 = (4 \times 16) + (4 \times \frac{1}{2})$

28. CORRECT ANSWER: C

$\dfrac{3}{4} = \dfrac{6}{8}$; $\dfrac{3.4}{.2} = \dfrac{34}{2} = 17$

29. CORRECT ANSWER: C

(A) $\begin{array}{r} 10 \times 15 = 150 \\ 2 \times 15 = \ \ 30 \\ \hline 180 \end{array}$ (B) $\begin{array}{r} 2 \times 15 = \ \ 30 \\ 10 \times 15 = 150 \\ \hline 180 \end{array}$ (C) $\begin{array}{r} 2 \times 15 = \ \ 30 \\ 10 \times 15 = 150 \\ \hline 180 \end{array}$

The Distributive Law links the operations of addition and
arithmetic.

30. CORRECT ANSWER: B
Partial Sums

```
      36        (A)  11      (C)  11      (D)  36
     +25            +20          +30          +20
     ───            ───          ───          ───
      61             31           41           56
                    +30          +20          + 5
                    ───          ───          ───
                     61           61           61
```

31. CORRECT ANSWER: A
100,000 × 10 = 1,000,000

32. CORRECT ANSWER: B
Division is repeated subtraction

```
                      21   quotient
divisor    12)256          dividend
               24
               ──
               16   minuend - partial dividend
               12
               ──
                4   partial dividend
```

```
    36   multiplicand              5   addend
  × 45   multiplier              +6   addend
  ────                           ──
   180   partial product         11   sum
   144   partial product
  ────
  1620   product
```

```
  7,485   minuend
 -2,648   subtrahend
 ──────
  4,837   remainder (difference)
```

33. CORRECT ANSWER: C
```
   $600          $480          $600          $480
 × .20         × .20         - 120         -  96
 ──────        ──────        ─────         ─────
 120.00         96.00         $480          $384  approximately
```

34. CORRECT ANSWER: C
```
Cost of one dozen        $33.00          $2.50
Selling price of one                     ×  12
    dozen                 30.00         $30.00  (sold at close-out sale)
Loss                    $ 3.00
```

$$\frac{L}{C} = \frac{\$3}{\$33} = \frac{1}{11} = 9\ 1/11\%$$

35. CORRECT ANSWER: B

SOLUTION

```
  10:56 A.M.                Add 3 hours, 58 minutes
  11:00 A.M.                            54 minutes
 + 3:00 hours               (see 10:56 A.M.)
 ─────────
  2:00 P.M.
 +  :54 minutes
 ──────────
  2:54 P.M.
```

36. CORRECT ANSWER: C

15¢	31¢	$7.33	$20.00
11¢	×3	+ .93	− 8.26
5¢	93¢	$8.26	$11.74
31¢			

37. CORRECT ANSWER: C

$30.19	$150.95	(amount on $5000)
× 5	+ 15.10	(amount on $500)
$150.95	$166.05	(approximately)

38. CORRECT ANSWER: C
1 cup = 8 oz.
1 quart = 4 cups (4 × 8 oz. = 32 oz.)
1 gallon = 32 oz. × 4 = 128 oz.
(1 gallon = 4 qts. or 128 oz.)
½ gallon = 64 oz.

```
   128 oz.
 + 64 oz.
6│ 192
   32 cups
```

39. CORRECT ANSWER: B

Cost	=	$36.00
10% of cost	=	3.60
Profit	=	9.00
Selling Price	=	$48.60

Selling price	=	$48.60
Cost	=	36.00
Markup	=	$12.60

$$\frac{Markup}{Cost} = \frac{\$12.60}{\$36.00} = 35\%$$

40. CORRECT ANSWER: C

1st carton

V = 8

2nd carton

V = 3

$$\frac{V1}{V2} = \frac{8}{3}$$

41. CORRECT ANSWER: A
    Step (1) Principal = $300
              Interest = $18 in 9 months (9 months = 3/4 year)

              To find annual interest:
                Let x = annual interest
                  3/4x = 18
                     x = 18 × 4/3
                     x = $24

              To find rate:
                Let R = rate

                  $R = \dfrac{I}{P} = \dfrac{24}{300} \begin{array}{l}\text{interest} \\ \text{principal}\end{array} \times$ 1 (year)

$$\begin{array}{r}.08 \\ 300\ )\overline{24.00} \\ \underline{24\ 00} \\ 00\end{array}$$

              Interest rate = 8%

    Step (2) Principal (?) to be invested at 8% to yield $120
              interest in 6 months:
              6 months = ½ year
              Yearly interest = $240 ($120 × 2)

              $P = \dfrac{I}{R}$

              $P = \dfrac{\$240}{.08} \begin{array}{l}\text{(interest)} \\ \text{(rate)}\end{array}$

              .08P = $240

$$.08\ )\overline{240}\ \ = \ 8\ )\overline{24000}^{\,3000}$$

              P = $3000 (the amount of money that would have to
                        be invested)

42. CORRECT ANSWER: C
    26 × 10 = $2.60 + .50 = $3.10

43. CORRECT ANSWER: C
    (approximately) 300 × 1,000 = 300,000

44.   CORRECT ANSWER: C

$$C = \pi D$$

$$C = \frac{22}{7} \times 28 = 88"$$

1 revolution of wheel covers 88"

$\dfrac{1}{12} \times 5280 \times \dfrac{12}{1}$ = traveling distance in inches

6 × 5280 = 31680 inches

```
        360  revolutions
88 )31680
    264
    ‾‾‾‾
    528
    528
    ‾‾‾‾
```

45.   CORRECT ANSWER: D

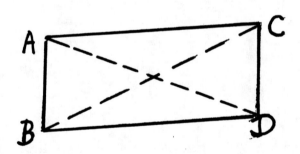

triangle = 180°

parallelogram = 360°

46.   CORRECT ANSWER: C
Division is repeated subtraction
Below is a division *pyramid*, which shows what actually happens
when we divide.

```
        8
       10
      200
32 )6985        dividend
   6400
   ‾‾‾‾
    585         partial dividend
    320
    ‾‾‾
    265         partial dividend
    256
    ‾‾‾
      9         partial dividend
```

   · 32 × 100 = 3200
     32 × 200 = 6400
     32 × 10 = 320

47. CORRECT ANSWER: B
     Diameter of moon = 2000 miles
     Diameter of earth = 8000 miles

MOON

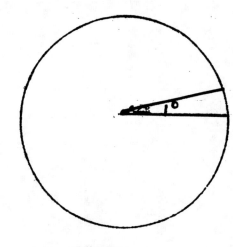

EARTH

The larger the circle,
the larger the arc.

$1°$ of arc $= \dfrac{1}{360}$ of

circle.

Circumference of earth = 25,000 miles
Circumference of moon = 6,200 miles (¼ of earth)

$$\begin{array}{r} 69+ \\ 360\overline{)25,000} \\ \underline{21\ 6} \\ 3\ 40 \\ \underline{3\ 24} \\ \overline{16} \end{array}$$

$1°$ = 69+ miles on the equator (Earth)
$1°$ = 17+ miles (Moon)

48. CORRECT ANSWER: C
     M   = 1000
     CM   = 900
     L   =   50
     VIII =   8
            ──────
            1958

49. CORRECT ANSWER: A

$\dfrac{2 + 2}{3 + 2} = \dfrac{4}{5} = \dfrac{12}{15}$

$\dfrac{2}{3} = \dfrac{10}{15}$

50. CORRECT ANSWER: B

$C = \dfrac{5}{9} (74 - 32)$ $C = \dfrac{5}{9} \times \dfrac{42}{1} = \dfrac{70}{3}$

$ = \dfrac{5}{9} (42)$ $ = 23\ 1/3°$

───

INTERPRETING STATISTICAL DATA
GRAPHS, CHARTS AND TABLES

Graphs, Charts, and Tables help us to visualize and to understand more readily ideas that might otherwise be more difficult to grasp.

The language of pictures is one of the oldest and easiest to understand.

There are several types of graphs.

The *pictograph* is used to compare numerical quantities. Symbols or pictures are used to represent numbers. Each symbol or picture represents a certain number of the quantities being compared.

The *bar graph* is employed to emphasize comparisons between numbers. If the graph is constructed of vertical bars, it is called a *vertical bar graph*. A fundamental part of this graph is the scale, which must begin with zero (0). In addition, a title heads this type of graph.

A *horizontal bar graph* employs horizontal bars. Here, too, the scale begins with zero (0), and there is a title.

The *line graph* shows how a quantity, such as prices, sales, temperature, rises or falls or changes. This type of graph is particularly good for delineating when the quantity is increasing and when it is decreasing. It also strikingly reveals trends or situations.

The *circle graph* is also used to show comparisons, particularly, the relationship between a whole thing and a part of the thing. The whole thing is represented by the circle, which is divided into pieces, called sectors, by the drawing of radii which form central angles. In order to find the number of degrees in the central angle of each sector, the method is to ascertain the fraction of the whole which the sector represents and to multiply by 360°.

———

Charts and tables also are used to visualize and to concretize facts and figures, to lead to comparisons, and to draw conclusions. Careful reading of the directions given with the charts or tables and of the questions employed in connection therewith, make these visual devices clear and meaningful as the student or candidate learns to be precise and resourceful in his reading and interpretation.

The Tests with questions that follow are intended to guide the candidate into the amazing world of graphs, charts and tables and to point up the importance of the quantitative ability to interpret statistical data.

EXAMINATION SECTION

TEST 1

The following graph represents the national debt of the United States from the year 1941 through the year 1950.

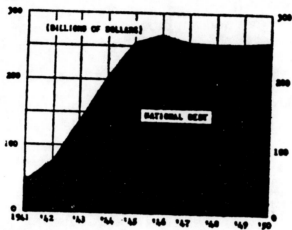

(BILLIONS OF DOLLARS)

NATIONAL DEBT

From this graph determine the answers to the following questions:
1. How many years are represented by the graph?
2. In what year was our national debt the smallest?
3. What was the national debt in 1944?
4. What was the approximate increase in the national debt from 1943 to 1944?
5. In what year was our national debt the largest?
6. In what year did the national debt begin to decrease?
7. How much greater was the national debt in 1950 than it was in 1941?
8. In what two consecutive years was the national debt the same?

TEST 2

The following pictorgram represents the number of telephones in use in a certain city. Each complete symbol represents 20,000 telephones.

1. How many telephones were in use in this city in 1985?
2. How many more telephones were in use in this city in 1985 than in 1975?
3. Find the per cent of increase in the number of telephones in use in 1990 over the number in use in 1970.
4. If it is estimated that 280,000 telephones will be in use in 1995, how many symbols should be used to picture this on the graph?

TEST 3

The following graph shows the noon temperature at a certain weather station on seven consecutive days in June.

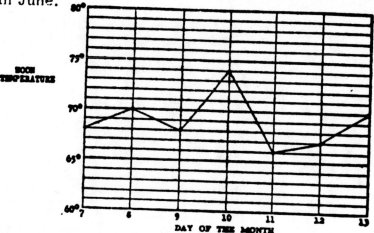

1. On what day was the noon temperature the highest?
2. For what two consecutive days was the change in noon temperature the least?
3. For what two consecutive days was the change in noon temperature the greatest?
4. What was the average noon temperature for the week?
5. How many degrees warmer was it at noon on June 9 than at noon on June 12?

TEST 4

The graph below shows food expenditures in the United States for each of the years 1970 to 1990 inclusive.

1. During what year were expenditures for food the lowest?
2. During what year were expenditures for food the highest?
3. Approximately how many billions of dollars were spent for food in 1980?
4. In what year did expenditures for food first reach 40 billion?
5. During which one of these five-year periods (1970-75, 1975-80, 1980-85, 1985-1990) did expenditures for food remain about the same?

TEST 5

In a recent year a large industrial concern used each dollar of its sales income as shown in the graph below.

Use in the business.......
Cash dividends ....
Depreciation ....
Direct taxes ....
Materials and services....
Wages and benefits.......

0 5 10 15 20 25 30 35 40 45
Amount in cents

1. How many cents of each dollar of sales income did the company use to pay wages and benefits?
2. How many more cents out of each sales dollar was spent on wages and benefits than on materials and services?
3. What was the total number of cents out of each sales dollar that the company set aside for depreciation and for use in the business?
4. The amount the company paid in direct taxes was how many times the amount it paid in cash dividends?
5. What per cent of each sales dollar was paid in cash dividends?

TEST 6

The circle graph below shows how the wage earners in a certain city earned their living in a recent year. The number of degrees required for each angle is given on the graph. Using the number of degrees shown on this graph,

1. find the fractional part of the graph that represents the number of wage earners earning their living in each of the following:
    (1) Trade and finance
    (2) Personal services
    (3) Manufacturing
2. How many times as many persons worked in the area of trade and finance as in the area of personal services?
3. If there were 180,000 wage earners in the city that year, how many persons were engaged in transportation?

4

TEST 7

RELATION BETWEEN CAR SPEED AND TIRE WEAR

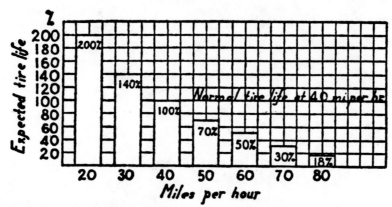

The graph above appeared in a magazine advertisement. Use the graph to answer the following:
1. At what speed is the normal life of a tire determined?
2. The life of a tire on a car driven at 20 miles per hour is how many times greater than the life of a tire on a car driven at 40 miles per hour?
3. What car speed will result in tires lasting only half of their normal tire life?
4. If a car is driven at 30 miles per hour, what per cent more than normal tire life may be expected?
5. If a car is driven at 70 miles per hour, what per cent less than normal tire life may be expected?

TEST 8

The graphs below were published by the federal government to show where the tax dollar comes from and where it goes.

Use the graphs above to answer the following questions:
1. What per cent of the federal tax dollar was spent on national security?
2. What per cent more money was obtained from individual income taxes than from corporation income taxes?
3. How many dollars, of every million dollars collected in taxes, were obtained from excise taxes?
4. List the four sources of income whose total approximately equals the amount spent for national security.

TEST 9

A savings bank in a large city published the graph below for its depositors. Use the graph to answer the following questions:

HOW YOUR SAVINGS WORK FOR YOU

61.6%
MORTGAGES

5.2% OTHER BONDS
3.4% CASH
24.7% U.S. BONDS
3.3% PREFERRED STOCK
1.8% ALL OTHER ASSETS

1. In what one way is approximately one fourth of the bank's assets invested?
2. Which fraction is nearest to the bank's total investment in mortgages: 1/2, 3/4, 5/8 ?
3. The bank's total assets are $162,575,800. Of this total, what amount is kept in cash?
4. Approximately how many times as much money is invested in United States Bonds as in other bonds?

TEST 10

The graph below appeared in a recent publication.

Growth in Motor Vehicle Registration since 1950

MOTOR VEHICLES REGISTERED IN MILLIONS

1950 55 60 65 70 75 80 85 90 95

1. Approximately how many motor vehicles were registered in 1985?
2. Approximately how many times as many motor vehicles were registered in 1985 as in 1955?
3. According to the estimate made on this graph, how many more motor vehicles will be registered in 1995 than in 1985?
4. What percent of increase in registration is expected between 1985 and 1995?

6

TEST 11

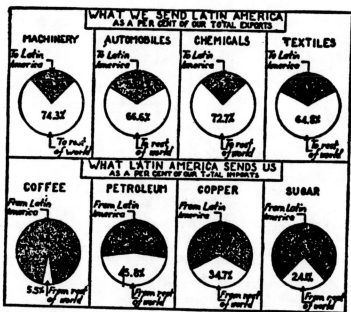

These items are based on the above graphs. On the line at the right of each of the following statements or questions, write the number preceding the word or expression that best completes the statement or answers the question.

1. The greatest export of the United States to Latin America is
    1. automobiles 2. chemicals 3. machinery 4. textiles a. ____

2. Latin America's greatest export to the United States is
    1. coffee 2. sugar 3. copper 4. petroleum b. ____

3. Products exported by the United States to Latin America are chiefly
    1. agricultural 2. manufactured 3. mineral 4. forest c. ____

4. As compared with Latin America's export trade to the United States , the export trade of the United States to Latin America is 1. greater 2. a little less 3. about the same 4. much less d. ____

5. Which statement concerning the foreign trade of the United States is true?
    (1) Most of our chemical exports go to areas other than Latin America.
    (2) Most of our automobile exports go to Latin America.
    (3) Most of our petroleum imports come from areas other than Latin America.
    (4) All of our coffee imports come from Latin America. e. ____

TEST 12

Last winter in a certain school, grades 2, 3, 4, 5 and 6 decided to get together supplies to send to needy children in other parts of the world.   The total amount collected was 720 pounds.

1. Copy on your answer paper the table above. which shows the number of pounds collected by each grade.   Then complete the table by writing for each grade the letter that indicates on the graph the fractional part of the total that was collected by that grade.
   (1) Grade 2:   180 pounds =
   (2) Grade 3:   90 pounds =
   (3) Grade 4:   120 pounds =
   (4) Grade 5:   60 pounds =
   (5) Grade 6:   270 pounds =
2. How many degrees are there in each section of the circle, A, B, C, D and E?

TEST 13

The accompanying pictograph shows the growth in production of a shoe company for the period 1978-1984   [Each symbol represents 20, 000 pairs of shoes.]
Using the pictograph, answer the following:

1. How many times as many shoes were produced in 1983 as in 1978?
2. How many pairs of shoes were produced in 1982?
3. How many more shoes were produced in 1984 than in 1983?

KEYS (CORRECT ANSWERS)/SOLUTIONS

TEST 1

1. 10 (1941 through 1950)
2. 1941 (slightly below 50 billions of dollars as indicated on the graph)
3. 200 billion dollars (the line graph for the year 1944 touches exactly on the 200 billion dollar mark)
4. approximately 60-65 billion dollars (200 billion dollars in 1944 minus approximately 135 to 140 billions in 1943)
5. 1946 (approximately 265 billion dollars)
6. 1946 (the line graph begins to decline starting in this year)
7. approximately 5 times greater (national debt in 1950 approximately 250 billion dollars ; national debt in 1941, approximately 50 billion dollars)
8. 1948, 1949 (the line graph does not change for these years)

TEST 2

1. 220,000 (20,000 x 11 = 220,000)
2. 50,000 (20,000 x 2 1/2)
3. 25% or 25

    (Each symbol = 20,000

    2 1/2 symbols = 50,000

    $\dfrac{50,000}{200,000}$ (1930 has 10 symbols) = $\dfrac{1}{4}$ or 25%)

4. 14 (280,000 ÷ 20,000)

TEST 3

1. 10th (74°)
2. 11th and the 12th (on these days the temperature rose from 66° to 67°, a change of 1°)
3. the 10th and the 11th (as shown by the steepest line, when the temperature fell from 74° to 66°, a change of 8°)
4. 69° (adding the temperatures from June 7 to June 13, we get 483°; dividing by 7, we find the average to be 69°)
5. 1° (noon temperature, June 9: 68°; noon temperature, June 12: 67°)

TEST 4

1. 1973 (low point of about 8 billion dollars in this year)
2. 1988 (high point of about 52 billion dollars in this year)
3. 50 (approximately 50 billion dollars)
4. 1986 (graph crosses the 40 billion dollar line in this year)
5. 1975-80 (graph line relatively stable for this period)

TEST 5

1. 40 (the bottom bar, which represents wages and benefits, reaches the 40-cent line)
2. 15 (40, representing wages and benefits, minus 25, representing materials and services)
3. 15 (10, representing depreciation, plus 5, representing use in the business)
4. 3 (15 represents direct taxes and 5 represents cash dividends, a ratio of 3 to 1)
5. 5 ($\dfrac{5}{100}$ = 5%)

TEST 6

1.(1) 1/4 ($\dfrac{90°}{360°}$ = 1/4)

   (2) 1/8 ($\dfrac{45°}{360°}$ = 1/8)

   (3) 1/3 ($\dfrac{120°}{360°}$ = 1/3)

2. 2 ($\dfrac{90°}{45°}$ = 2)

3. 10,000 ($\dfrac{20°}{360°}$ x 180,000)

TEST 7

1. 40 miles per hour (as stated in the graph proper)
2. 2 (at 20 miles per hour: expected tire life, 200%; at 40 miles per hour: expected tire life, 100%)
3. 60 miles per hour (as indicated on the graph)
4. 40% (as stated in the graph, 140% or 40% more than normal tire life (100%))
5. 70% (at 70 miles per hour: expected tire life, 30%; this is 70% less than normal tire life (100%).)

TEST 8

1. 68% $(\frac{68}{100} = 68\%)$
2. 12% (43 - 31 = 12¢ on each dollar or 12%)
3. 160,000 (1,000,000 x .16 = 160,000)
4. borrowing, excise taxes, customs and other taxes, individual income taxes (.04 + .16 + .06 + .43 = .69 (cost of national security, .68))

TEST 9

1. U.S. Bonds (24.7%)
2. 5/8 (61.6% is close to 62.5% or 5/8)
3. $5,527,577.20 (162,575,800 x 3.4% or .034)
4. 5 (approximately 25% ÷ approximately 5%)

TEST 10

1. 60 million (as indicated on the graph as registered)
2. 3 (60 ÷ 20)
3. 20 million (80 million - 60 million)
4. 33 1/3 (20 million/60 million = $\frac{1}{3}$ = 33 1/3%)

TEST 11

1. 4
2. 1
3. 2
4. 4
5. 1

TEST 12

1. (1) 180 pounds = A (second largest angle in the circle)
   (2) 90 pounds = C (fourth largest angle in the circle)
   (3) 120 pounds = E (third largest angle in the circle)
   (4) 60 pounds = D (smallest angle in the circle)
   (5) 270 pounds = B (the largest angle in the circle)

2. A = 90° $(\frac{180}{720} = \frac{1}{4})$

   B = 135° $(\frac{270}{720} = \frac{3}{8})$

   C = 45° $(\frac{90}{720} = \frac{1}{8})$

   D = 30° $(\frac{60}{720} = \frac{1}{12})$

   E = 60° $(\frac{120}{720} = \frac{1}{6})$

TEST 13

1. 10 (10 to 1)
2. 120,000 (6 x 20,000)
3. 50,000 (2 1/2 x 20,000)

EXAMINATION SECTION

DIRECTIONS: Each question or incomplete statement is followed by two suggested answers or completions. Select A or B, or C if the two figures have the same value, as the BEST answer that completes the statement or completes the statement. *PRINT THE LETTER OF THE CORRECT ANSWER IN THE SPACE AT THE RIGHT.*

1.

With which windlass can a man raise the heavier weight?

1.___

2.

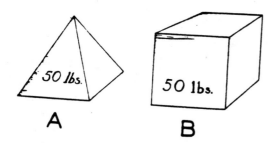

Which of these solid blocks will be the harder to tip over?

2.___

3.

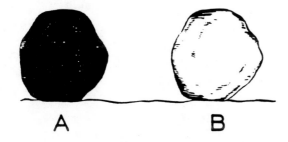

Which rock will get hotter in the sun?

3.___

4.

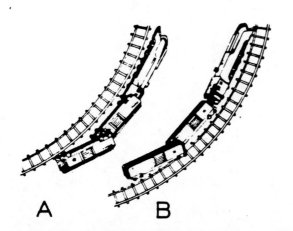

Which of these is the more likely picture of a train wreck?

4.___

5.

If the track is exactly level, on which rail does more pressure come?

5.___

6.

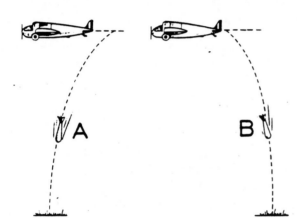

Which picture shows the way a bomb falls from a moving airplane if there is no wind?

6.___

7.

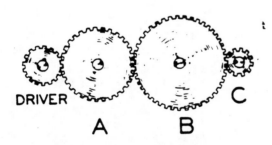

Indicate a gear which turn the same direction as the driver.

7.___

8.

If there are no clouds, on which night will you be able to see more stars?

8.___

9.

This wrench can be used to turn the pipe in direction:

9.___

10.

In which direction does the water in the right-hand pipe go?

10.___

11.

Which weighs more?

11.___

12.

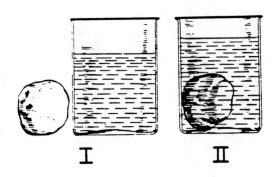

If the rock and tank of water together in picture I weigh 100 pounds, what will they weigh in picture II?

12.___

13.

A   B

Which steel wheel will
keep going longer after
the power has been shut
off?

13.___

14.

The top of the wheel *X*
will go
   A. steadily to the right
   B. steadily to the left
   C. by jerks to the left

14.___

15.

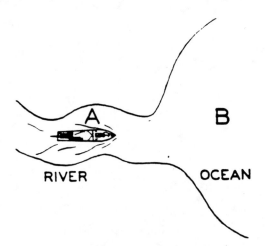

RIVER   OCEAN

At which point will the
boat be lower in the
water?

15.___

16.

Which arrow shows the way
the air will move along
the floor when the radiator
is turned on?

16.___

17.

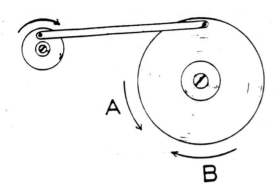

When the little wheel   17.___
turns around, the big
wheel will
    A. turn in direction A
    B. turn in direction B
    C. move back and forth

18.

Which boy gets more light   18.___
on the pages of his book?

19.

Which weighs more?   19.___

20.

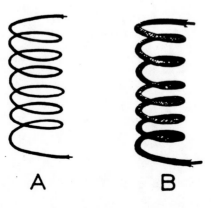

Which of these wires   20.___
offers more resistance to
the passage of an electric
current?

21.

Which spot on the wheel travels faster?

21.___

22.

With which arrangement can a man lift the heavier weight?

22.___

23.

Which room has more of an echo?

23.___

24.

Which would be the BETTER shears for cutting metal?

24.___

KEY (CORRECT ANSWERS)

1.	A	11.	B
2.	A	12.	C
3.	A	13.	B
4.	A	14.	C
5.	B	15.	A
6.	A	16.	A
7.	B	17.	C
8.	B	18.	A
9.	A	19.	A
10.	A	20.	A

21.	A
22.	C
23.	A
24.	B

―――――

NONVERBAL REASONING

DIRECTIONS: In each question, there are five drawings (A-E presented from left to right).
One drawing does NOT belong with the other four. You are to decide which drawing does NOT belong and PRINT THE LETTER of that drawing on your answer sheet.

EXAMPLES

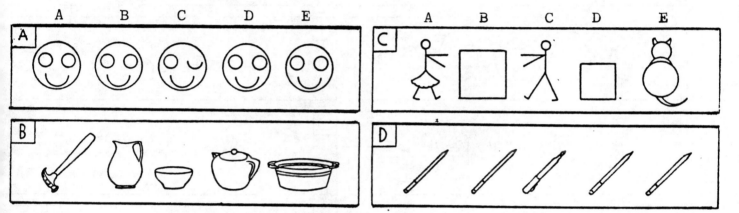

EXAMPLE A:
C does NOT belong because the eye is incomplete.

EXAMPLE B:
A does not belong because it is a hammer and the rest are objects relating to food.

EXAMPLE C:
E does not belong because while there are 2 each of the straight stick figures and squares, there is only one cat made of circular strokes.

EXAMPLE D:
C does not belong because it is thicker than the other pens, has a clip on its cap and it is a fountain pen while the rest are ballpoint pens.

KEY (CORRECT ANSWERS)

1.	C	21.	C	41.	C
2.	E	22.	E	42.	B
3.	C	23.	C	43.	E
4.	C	24.	C	44.	E
5.	C	25.	C	45.	B
6.	B	26.	B	46.	A
7.	C	27.	D	47.	C
8.	E	28.	A	48.	C
9.	B	29.	A	49.	E
10.	D	30.	D	50.	C
11.	D	31.	E	51.	C
12.	D	32.	B	52.	C
13.	E	33.	A	53.	A
14.	D	34.	D	54.	D
15.	D	35.	C	55.	D
16.	D	36.	C	56.	C
17.	D	37.	D	57.	A
18.	D	38.	A	58.	A
19.	E	39.	D	59.	B
20.	D	40.	B	60.	D

ABSTRACT REASONING
SPATIAL RELATIONS/TWO DIMENSIONS

COMMENTARY

Since intelligence exists in many forms or phases and the theory
of differential aptitudes is now firmly established in testing, other
manifestations and measurements of intelligence than verbal or purely
arithmetical must be identified and measured.

The spatial relations test, including that phase designated as spatial perception, involves and measures the ability to solve problems,
drawn up in the form of outlines or pictures, which are concerned with
the shapes of objects or the interrelationship of their parts. While,
concededly, little is known about the nature and scope of this aptitude,
it appears that this ability is required in science, mathematics, en-
gineering, and drawing courses and curricula. Accordingly, tests of
spatial perception involving the reconstruction of two-dimensional patterns, are presented in this section.

It is to be noted that the relationships expressed in spatial tests
are geometric, definitive, and exact. Keeping these basic characteristics in mind, the applicant is to proceed to solve the spatial perception problems in his own way. There is no set method of solving these
problems. The examinee may find that there are different methods for
different types of spatial problems. Therefore, the BEST way to prepare for this type of test is to *TAKE* and study the work-practice problems in two-dimensional patterns provided in this section.

———

ABSTRACT REASONING
SPATIAL RELATIONS/TWO DIMENSIONS

·The tests of spatial relations that follow consist of items which involve the visualization of two dimensions.

Each of the items of these tests consists of a line of figures -- a complete figure on the left and four lettered alternatives of component parts on the right, only one of which can be fitted together exactly to form the complete figure on the left.

The candidate is then required to select that choice of component parts which could be fitted together to form the complete figure given at the left.

────

SAMPLE QUESTIONS AND EXPLANATIONS

DIRECTIONS: The items in this part constitute a test of spatial relations involving two dimensions. Each item consists of a line of figures. The first figure is the complete figure. This is followed by four lettered choices of component parts, only one of which can be fitted together exactly to form the first (complete) figure.
Rules to be followed:
    1. The lettered choice of component parts selected as the answer must have the same number of parts as the first (complete) figure.
    2. The parts must fit exactly.
    3. The parts may be turned around but may not be turned over.

1.

The correct answer is D. When the two parts of D are completely closed, they form the complete figure on the left.

2.

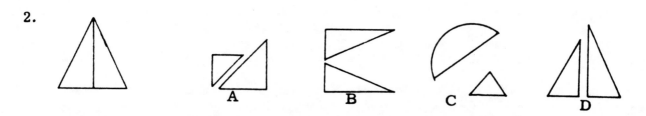

The correct answer is B. When the two parts of B are reversed in position, they form the complete figure on the left.

TEST 1

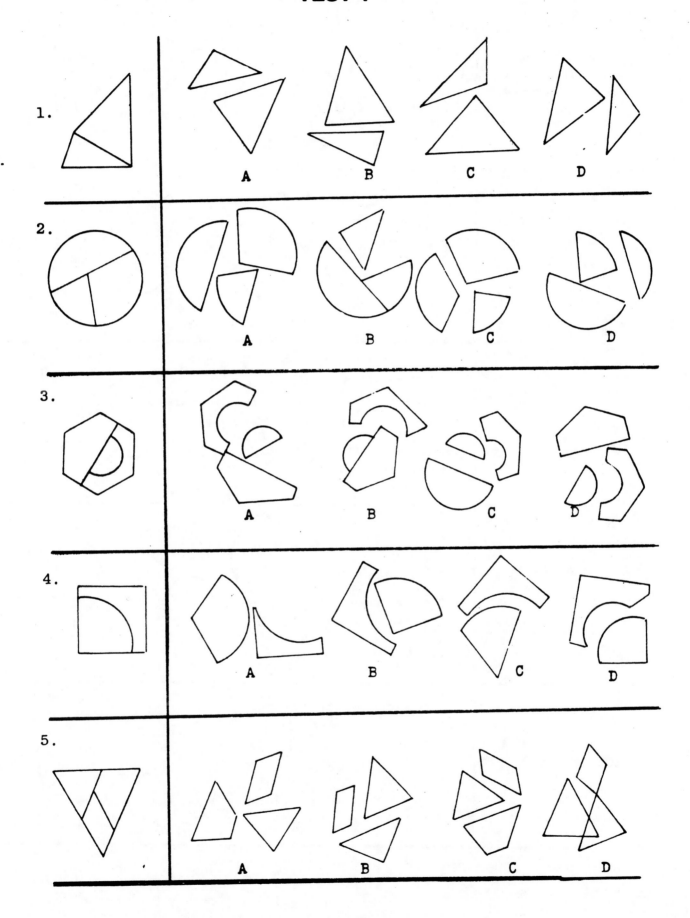

1.

A   B   C   D

2.

A   B   C   D

3.

A   B   C   D

4.

A   B   C   D

5.

A   B   C   D

3

TEST 3

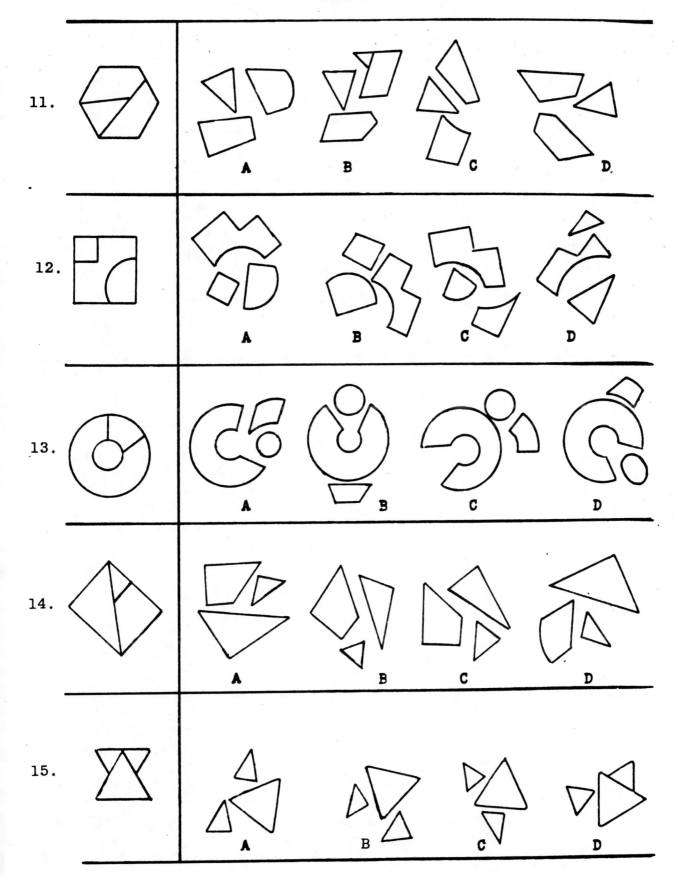

11.

    A   B   C   D

12.

    A   B   C   D

13.

    A   B   C   D

14.

    A   B   C   D

15.

    A   B   C   D

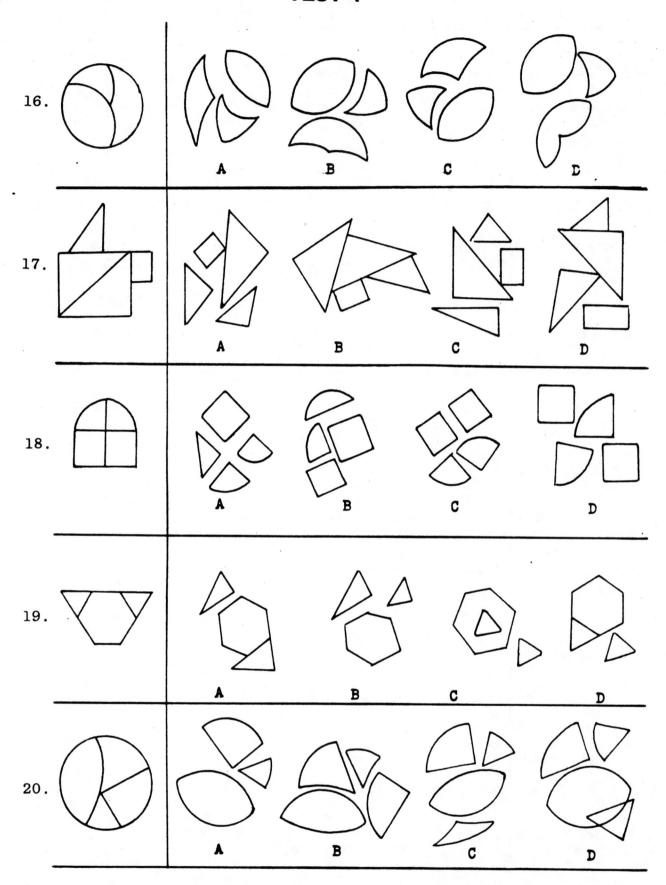

16.   A   B   C   D

17.   A   B   C   D

18.   A   B   C   D

19.   A   B   C   D

20.   A   B   C   D

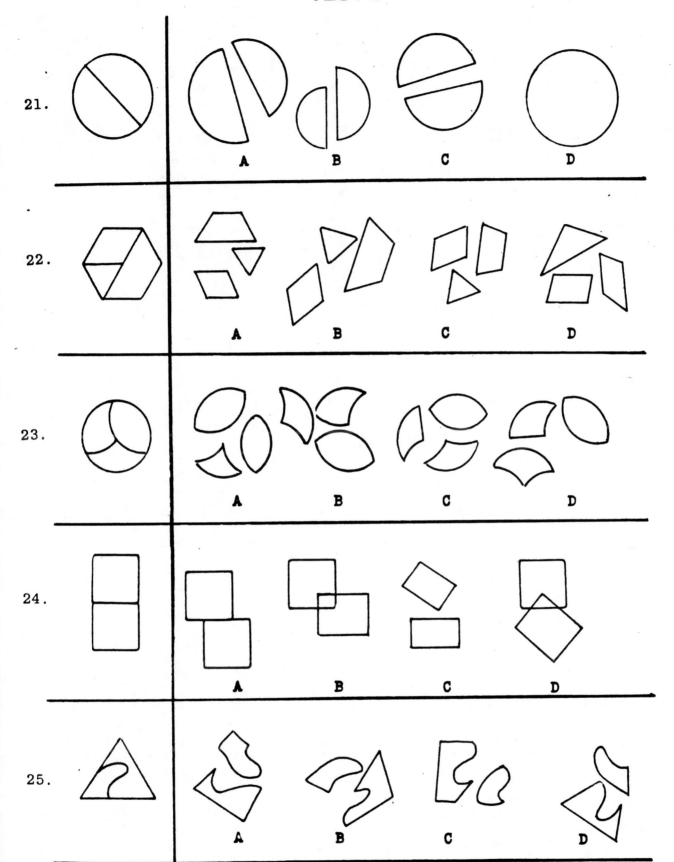

KEYS (CORRECT ANSWERS)

TEST 1	TEST 2	TEST 3	TEST 4	TEST 5
1. B	6. C	11. D	16. B	21. C
2. A	7. B	12. A	17. B	22. B
3. D	8. A	13. C	18. C	23. B
4. B	9. D	14. A	19. D	24. A
5. C	10. B	15. D	20. B	25. D

NUMBER SERIES PROBLEMS

COMMENTARY

Number series problems constitute an important means for measuring quantitative ability on the part of applicants for beginning and trainee positions as well as for regular, mid-level, and senior level positions.

In this method, numerical reasoning forms the primary technic for measuring mathematical ability.

This test measures your ability to think with numbers instead of words.

In each problem, you are given a series of numbers that are changing according to a rule - followed by five sets of 2 numbers each. Your problem is to figure out a rule that would make one of the five sets the next two numbers in the series.

The problems do not use hard arithmetic. The task is merely to see how the numbers are related to each other. The sample questions will explain several types in detail so that you may become familiar with what you have to do.

<u>HINTS FOR ANSWERING NUMBER SERIES QUESTIONS</u>

1. Do the ones that are easier for you *first*. Then go back and work on the others. Enough time is allowed for you to do all the questions, provided you don't stay too long on the ones you have trouble answering.

2. Sound out the series to yourself. You may hear the rule: 2 4 6 8 10 12 14 ... What are the next two numbers?

3. Look at the series carefully. You may see the rule: 9 2 9 4 9 6 9... What are the next two numbers?

4. If you can't hear it or see it, you may have to figure it out by writing down how the numbers are changing: 6 8 16 18 26 28 36 ... What are the next two numbers?

6^{+2} 8^{+8} 16^{+2} 18^{+8} 26^{+2} 28^{+8} 36... What are the next two numbers if this is +2 +8? 36 + 2 = 38 + 8 = 46 or 38 46. You would mark the letter of the answer that goes with 38 46.

5. If none of the answers given fits the rule you have figured out, try again. Try to figure out a rule that makes one of the five answers a correct one.

6. Don't spend too much time on any one question. Skip it and come back. A fresh look sometimes helps.

———

SAMPLE QUESTIONS

DIRECTIONS: In each of the questions in this test, there is at the top a series of numbers which follow some definite order and, below, five sets of two numbers each.

You are to look at the numbers in the series at the top and find out what order they follow. Then decide what the next two numbers in that series would be if the same order were continued. Next find these two numbers in one of the sets below. *PRINT THE LETTER OF THE CORRECT ANSWER IN THE SPACE AT THE RIGHT.*

1. 1 2 3 4 5 6 7 .....   1. ...
    A. 1 2   B. 5 6   C. 8 9   D. 4 5   E. 7 8
How are these numbers changing? The numbers in this series are increasing by 1 or the rule is "add 1." If you apply this rule to the series, what would the next two numbers be? 7 + 1 = 8 + 1 = 9. Therefore, the CORRECT answer is 8 and 9, and you would select C. 8 9 as your answer.

1

2. 15 14 13 12 11 10 9 ....   2. ..
    A. 2 1   B. 17 16   C. 8 9   D. 8 7   E. 9 8
The numbers in this series are decreasing by 1 or the rule is
"subtract 1." If you apply that rule, what would the next two
numbers be? $9 - 1 = 8 - 1 = 7$. The CORRECT answer is 8 and
7, and you would select D. 8 7 as your answer.

3. 20 20 21 21 22 22 23 ....   3. ..
    A. 23 23   B. 23 24   C. 19 19   D. 22 23   E. 21 22
In this series each number is repeated and then increased by
1. The rule is "repeat, add 1, repeat, add 1, etc." The se-
ries would be $20^{+0}20^{+1}21^{+0}21^{+1}22^{+0}22^{+1}23^{+0}23^{+1}24$. The CORRECT
answer is 23 and 24, and you should have selected B. 23 24 as
your answer.

4. 17 3 17 4 17 5 17 ....   4. ..
    A. 6 17   B. 6 7   C. 17 6   D. 5 6   E. 17 7
If you can't find a single rule for all the numbers in a series, see if there are really two series in the problem. This
series is the number 17 separated by numbers increasing by 1,
starting with 3. If the series were continued for two more
numbers, it would read 17 3 17 4 17 5 17 6 17. The CORRECT
answer is 6 and 17, and you should have selected A. 6 17 for
question 4.

5. 1 2 4 5 7 8 10 ....   5. ..
    A. 11 12   B. 12 14   C. 10 13   D. 12 13   E. 11 13
The rule in this series is not easy to see until you actually
set down how the numbers are changing: $1^{+1}2^{+2}4^{+1}5^{+2}7^{+1}8^{+2}10$.
The numbers in this series are increasing first by 1 (that is,
plus 1) and then by 2 (that is, plus 2). If the series were continued for two more numbers, it would read: 1 2 4 5 7 8 10
(plus 1) which is 11 (plus 2) which is 13. Therefore, the COR-
RECT answer is 11 and 13, and you should have selected E.
11 13 for question 5.

*NOW READ AND WORK SAMPLE QUESTIONS 6 THROUGH 10 AND MARK YOUR ANSWERS
IN THE SPACE PROVIDED AT THE RIGHT.*

6. 21 21 20 20 19 19 18 ....   6. ..
    A. 18 18   B. 18 17   C. 17 18   D. 17 17   E. 18 19
7. 1 22 1 23 1 24 1 ....   7. ..
    A. 26 1   B. 25 26   C. 25 1   D. 1 26   E. 1 25
8. 1 20 3 19 5 18 7 ....   8. ..
    A. 8 9   B. 8 17   C. 17 10   D. 17 9   E. 9 18
9. 4 7 10 13 16 19 22 ....   9. ..
    A. 23 26   B. 25 27   C. 25 26   D. 25 28   E. 24 27
10. 30 2 28 4 26 6 24 ....   10. ..
    A. 23 9   B. 26 8   C. 8 9   D. 26 22   E. 8 22

EXPLANATIONS FOR QUESTIONS 6 THROUGH 10.

6. Each number in the series repeats itself and then decreases by
1 or minus 1; 21 (repeat) 21 (minus 1) which makes 20 (repeat)
20 (minus 1) which makes 19 (repeat) 19 (minus 1) which makes
18 (repeat) ? (minus 1) ? The CORRECT answer is B.

7. The number 1 is separated by numbers which begin with 22 and increase by 1; 1 22 1 (increase 22 by 1) which makes 23 1 (increase
23 by 1) which makes 24 1 (increase 24 by 1) which makes ? The
CORRECT answer is C.

8. This is best explained by two alternating series - one series starts with 1 and increases by 2 or plus 2; the other series starts with 20 and decreases by 1 or minus 1. The CORRECT answer is D.

$$1\uparrow \ 3\uparrow \ 5\uparrow \ 7\uparrow \ ?$$
$$20 \ 19 \ 18 \ ?$$

9. This series of numbers increases by 3 (plus 3) beginning with the first number - 4 (plus 3) 7 (plus 3) 10 (plus 3) 13 (plus 3) 16 (plus 3) 19 (plus 3) 22 (plus 3) ? The CORRECT answer is D.

10. Look for two alternating series - one series starts with 30 and decreases by 2 (minus 2); the other series starts with 2 and increases by 2 (plus 2). The CORRECT answer is E.

$$30\uparrow \ 28\uparrow \ 26\uparrow \ 24\uparrow \ ?$$
$$2 \quad 4 \quad 6 \quad ?$$

KEY (CORRECT ANSWERS)

1. C	3. B	5. E	7. C	9. D
2. D	4. A	6. B	8. D	10. E

NUMBER SERIES PROBLEMS

DIRECTIONS FOR THIS SECTION:

In each of the questions in this test, there is at the top a series of numbers which follow some definite order and, below, five sets of two numbers each.

You are to look at the numbers in the series at the top and find out what order they follow. Then decide what the next two numbers in that series would be if the same order were continued. Next find these two numbers in one of the sets below. *PRINT THE LETTER OF THE CORRECT ANSWER IN THE SPACE AT THE RIGHT.*

TEST 1

1. 5 6 20 7 8 19 9 ....   1. ...
   A. 10 18   B. 18 17   C. 10 17   D. 18 19   E. 10 11
2. 9 10 1 11 12 2 13 ....   2. ...
   A. 2 14   B. 3 14   C. 14 3   D. 14 15   E. 14 1
3. 4 6 9 11 14 16 19 ....   3. ...
   A. 21 24   B. 22 25   C. 20 22   D. 21 23   E. 22 24
4. 8 8 1 10 10 3 12 ....   4. ...
   A. 13 13   B. 12 5   C. 12 4   D. 13 5   E. 4 12
5. 14 1 2 15 3 4 16 ....   5. ...
   A. 5 16   B. 6 7   C. 5 17   D. 5 6   E. 17 5
6. 10 12 50 15 17 50 20 ....   6. ...
   A. 50 21   B. 21 50   C. 50 22   D. 22 50   E. 22 24
7. 1 2 3 50 4 5 6 51 7 8 ....   7. ...
   A. 9 10   B. 9 52   C. 51 10   D. 10 52   E. 10 50
8. 20 21 23 24 27 28 32 33 38 39 ....   8. ...
   A. 45 46   B. 45 52   C. 44 45   D. 44 49   E. 40 46
9. 17 15 21 18 10 16 19 ....   9. ...
   A. 20 5   B. 5 11   C. 11 11   D. 11 20   E. 15 14
10. 12 16 10 14 8 12 6 ....   10. ...
    A. 10 14   B. 10 8   C. 10 4   D. 4 10   E. 4 2

TEST 2

1. 10 11 12 10 11 12 10 ....
    A. 10 11   B. 12 10   C. 11 10   D. 11 12   E. 10 12
2. 4 6 7 4 6 7 4
    A. 6 7   B. 4 7   C. 7 6   D. 7 4   E. 6 8
3. 7 7 3 7 7 4 7 ....
    A. 4 5   B. 4 7   C. 5 7   D. 7 5   E. 7 7
4. 3 4 10 5 6 10 7 ....
    A. 10 8   B. 9 8   C. 8 14   D. 8 9   E. 8 10
5. 6 6 7 7 8 8 9 ....
    A. 10 11   B. 10 10   C. 9 10   D. 9 9   E. 10 9
6. 3 8 9 4 9 10 5 ....
    A. 6 10   B. 10 11   C. 9 10   D. 11 6   E. 10 6
7. 2 4 3 6 4 8 5 ....
    A. 6 10   B. 10 7   C. 10 6   D. 9 6   E. 6 7
8. 11 5 9 7 7 9 5 ....
    A. 11 3   B. 7 9   C. 7 11   D. 9 7   E. 3 7
9. 12 10 8 8 6 4 4 ....
    A. 2 2   B. 6 4   C. 6 2   D. 4 6   E. 2 0
10. 20 22 22 19 21 21 18 ....
    A. 22 22   B. 19 19   C. 20 20   D. 20 17   E. 19 17

1. ...
2. ...
3. ...
4. ...
5. ...
6. ...
7. ...
8. ...
9. ...
10. ...

TEST 3

1. 5 7 6 10 7 13 8 ....
    A. 16 9   B. 16 10   C. 9 15   D. 10 15   E. 15 9
2. 13 10 11 15 12 13 17 ....
    A. 18 14   B. 18 15   C. 15 16   D. 14 15   E. 15 18
3. 30 27 24 21 18 15 12 ....
    A. 9 3   B. 9 6   C. 6 3   D. 12 9   E. 8 5
4. 3 7 10 5 8 10 7 ....
    A. 10 11   B. 10 5   C. 10 9   D. 10 10   E. 9 10
5. 12 4 13 6 14 8 15 ....
    A. 10 17   B. 17 10   C. 10 12   D. 16 10   E. 10 16
6. 21 8 18 20 7 17 19 ....
    A. 16 18   B. 18 6   C. 6 16   D. 5 15   E. 6 18
7. 14 16 16 18 20 20 22 ....
    A. 22 24   B. 26 28   C. 24 26   D. 24 24   E. 24 28
8. 5 6 8 9 12 13 17 ....
    A. 18 23   B. 13 18   C. 18 22   D. 23 24   E. 18 19
9. 1 3 5 5 2 4 6 6 3 ....
    A. 7 4   B. 5 5   C. 1 3   D. 5 7   E. 7 7
10. 12 24 15 25 18 26 21 ....
    A. 27 22   B. 24 22   C. 29 24   D. 27 27   E. 27 24

1. ...
2. ...
3. ...
4. ...
5. ...
6. ...
7. ...
8. ...
9. ...
10. ...

TEST 4

1. 8 9 9 8 10 10 8 ....
    A. 11 8   B. 8 13   C. 8 11   D. 11 11   E. 8 8
2. 10 10 11 11 12 12 13 ....
    A. 15 15   B. 13 13   C. 14 14   D. 13 14   E. 14 15
3. 6 6 10 6 6 12 6 ....
    A. 6 14   B. 13 6   C. 14 6   D. 6 13   E. 6 6

1. ...
2. ...
3. ...

4.   17 11 5 16 10 4 15 ....
    A. 13 9   B. 13 11   C. 8 5   D. 9 5   E. 9 3

5.   1 3 2 4 3 5 4 ....
    A. 6 8   B. 5 6   C. 6 5   D. 3 4   E. 3 5

6.   11 11 10 12 12 11 13 ....
    A. 12 14   B. 14 12   C. 14 14   D. 13 14   E. 13 12

7.   18 5 6 18 7 8 18 ....
    A. 9 9   B. 9 10   C. 18 9   D. 8 9   E. 18 7

8.   7 8 9 13 10 11 12 14 13 14 ....
    A. 15 16   B. 13 15   C. 14 15   D. 15 15   E. 13 14

9.   5 7 30 9 11 30 13 ....
    A. 15 16   B. 15 17   C. 14 17   D. 15 30   E. 30 17

10. 5 7 11 13 17 19 23 ....
    A. 27 29   B. 25 29   C. 25 27   D. 27 31   E. 29 31

4. ...
5. ...
6. ...
7. ...
8. ...
9. ...
10. ...

TEST 5

1.   9 15 10 17 12 19 15 21 19 ....
    A. 23 24   B. 25 23   C. 17 23   D. 23 31   E. 21 24

2.   34 37 30 33 26 29 22 ....
    A. 17 8   B. 18 11   C. 25 28   D. 25 20   E. 25 18

3.   10 16 12 14 14 12 16 ....
    A. 14 12   B. 10 18   C. 10 14   D. 14 18   E. 14 16

4.   11 12 18 11 13 19 11 14 ....
    A. 18 11   B. 16 11   C. 20 11   D. 11 21   E. 17 11

5.   20 9 8 19 10 9 18 11 10 ....
    A. 19 11   B. 17 10   C. 19 12   D. 17 12   E. 19 10

6.   28 27 26 31 30 29 34 ....
    A. 36 32   B. 32 31   C. 33 32   D. 33 36   E. 35 36

7.   10 16 14 20 18 24 22 ....
    A. 28 32   B. 27 26   C. 28 26   D. 26 28   E. 27 28

8.   9 9 7 8 7 7 9 10 5 ....
    A. 5 11   B. 11 12   C. 5 9   D. 9 11   E. 5 5

9.   5 7 11 17 10 12 16 22 15 17 ....
    A. 27 26   B. 19 23   C. 19 27   D. 21 23   E. 21 27

10. 12 19 13 20 14 21 15 ....
    A. 16 17   B. 22 16   C. 16 22   D. 15 22   E. 15 16

1. ...
2. ...
3. ...
4. ...
5. ...
6. ...
7. ...
8. ...
9. ...
10. ...

TEST 6

1.   13 12 8 11 10 8 9 ....
    A. 8 7   B. 6 8   C. 8 6   D. 8 8   E. 7 8

2.   13 18 13 17 13 16 13 ....
    A. 15 13   B. 13 14   C. 13 15   D. 14 15   E. 15 14

3.   13 13 10 12 12 10 11 ....
    A. 10 10   B. 10 9   C. 11 9   D. 9 11   E. 11 10

4.   6 5 4 6 5 4 6 ....
    A. 4 6   B. 6 4   C. 5 4   D. 5 6   E. 4 5

5.   10 10 9 8 8 7 6 ....
    A. 5 5   B. 5 4   C. 6 5   D. 6 4   E. 5 3

6.   20 16 18 14 16 12 14 ....
    A. 16 12   B. 10 12   C. 16 18   D. 12 12   E. 12 10

1. ...
2. ...
3. ...
4. ...
5. ...
6. ...

5

7.   7 12 8 11 9 10 10 ....
    A. 11 9   B. 9 8   C. 9 11   D. 10 11   E. 9 10   7. ..

8.   13 13 12 15 15 14 17 ....
    A. 17 16   B. 14 17   C. 16 19   D. 19 19   E. 16 16   8. ..

9.   19 18 12 17 16 13 15 ....
    A. 16 12   B. 14 14   C. 12 14   D. 14 12   E. 12 16   9. ..

10.   7 15 12 8 16 13 9 ....
    A. 17 14   B. 17 10   C. 14 10   D. 14 17   E. 10 14   10. ..

—

TEST 7

1.   18 15 6 16 14 6 14 ....
    A. 12 6   B. 14 13   C. 6 12   D. 13 12   E. 13 6   1. ..

2.   6 6 5 8 8 7 10 10 ....
    A. 8 12   B. 9 12   C. 12 12   D. 12 9   E. 9 9   2. ..

3.   17 20 23 26 29 32 35 ....
    A. 37 40   B. 41 44   C. 38 41   D. 38 42   E. 36 39   3. ..

4.   15 5 7 16 9 11 17 ....
    A. 18 13   B. 15 17   C. 12 19   D. 13 15   E. 12 13   4. ..

5.   19 17 16 16 13 15 10 ....
    A. 14 7   B. 12 9   C. 14 9   D. 7 12   E. 10 14   5. ..

6.   11 1 16 10 6 21 9 ....
    A. 12 26   B. 26 8   C. 11 26   D. 11 8   E. 8 11   6. ..

7.   21 21 19 17 17 15 13 ....
    A. 11 11   B. 13 11   C. 11 9   D. 9 7   E. 13 13   7. ..

8.   23 22 20 19 16 15 11 ....
    A. 6 5   B. 10 9   C. 6 1   D. 10 6   E. 10 5   8. ..

9.   17 10 16 9 14 8 11 ....
    A. 7 11   B. 7 7   C. 10 4   D. 4 10   E. 7 4   9. ..

10.   11 9 14 12 17 15 20 18 23 ....
    A. 21 24   B. 26 21   C. 21 26   D. 24 27   E. 26 29   10. ..

—

TEST 8

1.   13 4 5 13 6 7 13 ....
    A. 13 8   B. 8 13   C. 8 9   D. 8 8   E. 7 8   1. ..

2.   10 10 9 11 11 10 12 ....
    A. 13 14   B. 12 11   C. 13 13   D. 12 12   E. 12 13   2. ..

3.   6 6 8 10 10 12 14 ....
    A. 14 14   B. 14 16   C. 16 16   D. 12 14   E. 10 10   3. ..

4.   8 1 9 3 10 5 11 ....
    A. 7 12   B. 6 12   C. 12 6   D. 7 8   E. 6 7   4. ..

5.   30 11 24 12 19 14 15 17 12 21 10 ....
    A. 23 8   B. 25 8   C. 26 9   D. 24 9   E. 25 9   5. ..

6.   24 30 29 22 28 27 19 26 25 15 24 ....
    A. 14 23   B. 19 18   C. 23 22   D. 25 11   E. 23 10   6. ..

7.   7 5 9 7 11 9 13 ....
    A. 11 14   B. 10 15   C. 11 15   D. 12 14   E. 10 14   7. ..

8.   9 10 11 7 8 9 5 ....
    A. 6 7   B. 7 8   C. 5 6   D. 6 4   E. 7 5   8. ..

9.   8 9 10 10 9 10 11 11 10 11 12 ....
    A. 11 12   B. 12 10   C. 11 11   D. 12 11   E. 11 13   9. ..

10.   5 6 8 9 12 13 17 18 23 24 ....
    A. 30 31   B. 25 31   C. 29 30   D. 25 30   E. 30 37   10. ..

—

TEST 9

1. 8 9 10 8 9 10 8 ....
       A. 8 9   B. 9 10   C. 9 8   D. 10 8   E. 8 10

2. 3 4 4 3 5 5 3 ....
       A. 3 3   B. 6 3   C. 3 6   D. 6 6   E. 6 7

3. 7 7 3 7 7 4 7 ....
       A. 7 7   B. 7 8   C. 5 7   D. 8 7   E. 7 5

4. 18 18 19 20 20 21 22 ....
       A. 22 23   B. 23 24   C. 23 23   D. 22 22   E. 21 22

5. 2 6 10 3 7 11 4 ....
       A. 12 16   B. 5 9   C. 8 5   D. 12 5   E. 8 12

6. 11 8 15 12 19 16 23 ....
       A. 27 20   B. 24 20   C. 27 24   D. 20 24   E. 20 27

7. 16 8 15 9 14 10 13 ....
       A. 12 11   B. 13 12   C. 11 13   D. 11 12   E. 11 14

8. 4 5 13 6 7 12 8 ....
       A. 9 11   B. 13 9   C. 9 13   D. 11 9   E. 11 10

9. 3 8 4 9 5 10 6 11 7 ....
       A. 7 11   B. 7 8   C. 11 8   D. 12 7   E. 12 8

10. 18 14 19 17 20 20 21 ....
       A. 22 24   B. 14 19   C. 24 21   D. 21 23   E. 23 22

1. ...
2. ...
3. ...
4. ...
5. ...
6. ...
7. ...
8. ...
9. ...
10. ...

———

TEST 10

1. 6 9 10 7 11 12 8 ....
       A. 9 10   B. 9 13   C. 16 14   D. 13 14   E. 14 15

2. 7 5 3 9 7 5 11 ....
       A. 13 12   B. 7 5   C. 9 7   D. 13 7   E. 9 9

3. 7 9 18 10 12 18 13 ....
       A. 18 14   B. 15 18   C. 14 15   D. 15 14   E. 14 18

4. 2 6 4 8 6 10 8 ....
       A. 12 10   B. 6 10   C. 10 12   D. 12 16   E. 6 4

5. 7 9 12 14 17 19 22 ....
       A. 25 27   B. 23 24   C. 23 25   D. 24 27   E. 26 27

6. 3 23 5 25 7 27 9 ....
       A. 10 11   B. 27 29   C. 29 11   D. 11 28   E. 28 10

7. 18 17 16 14 13 12 10 ....
       A. 9 8   B. 6 7   C. 8 6   D. 8 7   E. 10 9

8. 5 7 8 10 11 13 14 16 ....
       A. 18 19   B. 17 18   C. 18 20   D. 17 19   E. 19 20

9. 28 27 25 24 22 21 19 ....
       A. 18 16   B. 17 16   C. 18 17   D. 17 15   E. 20 18

10. 2 2 4 6 6 8 10 ....
       A. 12 12   B. 12 14   C. 10 10   D. 10 8   E. 10 12

1. ...
2. ...
3. ...
4. ...
5. ...
6. ...
7. ...
8. ...
9. ...
10. ...

———

KEY (CORRECT ANSWERS)

TEST 1		TEST 2		TEST 3		TEST 4		TEST 5	
1.	A	1.	D	1.	A	1.	D	1.	A
2.	C	2.	A	2.	D	2.	D	2.	E
3.	A	3.	D	3.	B	3.	A	3.	B
4.	B	4.	E	4.	E	4.	E	4.	C
5.	D	5.	C	5.	E	5.	C	5.	D
6.	D	6.	B	6.	C	6.	E	6.	C
7.	B	7.	C	7.	D	7.	B	7.	C
8.	A	8.	A	8.	A	8.	D	8.	A
9.	B	9.	E	9.	D	9.	D	9.	E
10.	C	10.	C	10.	E	10.	B	10.	B

TEST 6		TEST 7		TEST 8		TEST 9		TEST 10	
1.	D	1.	E	1.	C	1.	B	1.	D
2.	A	2.	B	2.	B	2.	D	2.	C
3.	E	3.	C	3.	B	3.	E	3.	B
4.	C	4.	D	4.	A	4.	A	4.	A
5.	C	5.	A	5.	C	5.	E	5.	D
6.	B	6.	C	6.	E	6.	E	6.	C
7.	C	7.	B	7.	C	7.	D	7.	A
8.	A	8.	E	8.	A	8.	A	8.	D
9.	B	9.	B	9.	D	9.	E	9.	A
10.	A	10.	C	10.	A	10.	E	10.	E

ANSWER SHEET

NO. _____ PART _____ TITLE OF POSITION _____

ᴀCE OF EXAMINATION _____ DATE _____

(CITY OR TOWN)   (STATE)

RATING

USE THE SPECIAL PENCIL.   MAKE GLOSSY BLACK MARKS.

Make only ONE mark for each answer.   Additional and stray marks may be counted as mistakes.   In making corrections, erase errors COMPLETELY.

ANSWER SHEET

TEST NO. _____ PART _____ TITLE OF POSITION _____

PLACE OF EXAMINATION _____ DATE_____

(CITY OR TOWN)   (STATE)

RATING

USE THE SPECIAL PENCIL.   MAKE GLOSSY BLACK MARKS.

Make only ONE mark for each answer.   Additional and stray marks may be
counted as mistakes.   In making corrections, erase errors COMPLETELY.

(Answer grid, questions 1–125, columns A B C D E)